The Moroccan Argan Trade

This book provides one of the most detailed and comprehensive examinations of the Moroccan argan tree, the products derived from it and its cultural significance.

The Moroccan argan trade is booming, but as the tree provides important ecological functions and plays an important role, both financially and culturally, for the Amazigh (Berber) people it has become a key topic of debate. This book thoroughly examines the production stories, benefits and impacts and provides a value-chain analysis which compares different cooperatives and approaches to production. It assesses the fair-trade approaches and attempts at sustainable production of the bio-trade resource. While being a vital source of income, the argan tree has a significant cultural importance to the Indigenous people and the book assesses the impact of the argan trade on their well-being, community and livelihoods. It examines Indigenous knowledge and intellectual property issues relating to the trade, as well as Berber-state law and politics.

Assessing factors relating to legal and economic geography international trade, socio-cultural and human-nature relationships, the book provides a comprehensive analysis of the argan tree which will appeal to students, scholars and practitioners.

Daniel F. Robinson is Professor in the Environment and Society Group, Faculty of Arts and Social Sciences at the University of New South Wales (UNSW), Australia. He is also Academic Lead for the Pacific Region for the UNSW Institute for Global Development and has acted as a researcher and policy advisor for the Access and Benefit-Sharing Capacity Development Initiative, United Nations Development Programme (UNDP), International Centre for Trade and Sustainable Development (ICTSD) and several other development programs and environmental agencies. He is the author of *Biodiversity, Access and Benefit-Sharing: Global Case Studies* (Routledge, 2015) and lead editor of *Protecting Traditional Knowledge* (Routledge, 2017).

Earthscan Studies in Natural Resource Management

Social Movements Contesting Natural Resource Development
Edited by John F. Devlin

Benefit-sharing in Environmental Governance
Local Experiences of a Global Concept
Louisa Parks

Governing Renewable Natural Resources
Theories and Frameworks
Edited by Fiona Nunan

Interdisciplinary Collaboration for Water Diplomacy
A Principled and Pragmatic Approach
Edited by Shafiqul Islam and Kevin M. Smith

Peatlands
Ecology, Conservation and Heritage
Ian D. Rotherham

The Moroccan Argan Trade
Producer Networks and Human Bio-Geographies
Daniel F. Robinson

For more information on books in this series, please visit: http://www.routledge.com/books/series/ECNRM/

The Moroccan Argan Trade

Producer Networks and Human Bio-Geographies

Daniel F. Robinson

LONDON AND NEW YORK

First published 2020
by Routledge
2 Park Square, Milton Park, Abingdon, Oxon OX14 4RN

and by Routledge
605 Third Avenue, New York, NY 10017

First issued in paperback 2021

Routledge is an imprint of the Taylor & Francis Group, an informa business

British Library Cataloguing-in-Publication Data
A catalogue record for this book is available from the British Library

Library of Congress Cataloging-in-Publication Data
Names: Robinson, Daniel F., author.
Title: The Moroccan argan trade : producer networks and human bio-geographies / Daniel F. Robinson.
Description: New York : Routledge, 2020. | Includes bibliographical references and index.
Identifiers: LCCN 2019058591 (print) | LCCN 2019058592 (ebook) | ISBN 9780367423599 (hardback) | ISBN 9780367853556 (ebook)
Subjects: LCSH: Berbers—Morocco—Economic conditions. | Women, Berber—Morocco—Economic conditions. | Berbers—Social life and customs. | Oil industries—Morocco. | Argania spinosa—Morocco. | Cultural property—Protection—Law and legislation—Morocco.
Classification: LCC DT313.2 .R63 2020 (print) | LCC DT313.2 (ebook) | DDC 305.89330964—dc23
LC record available at https://lccn.loc.gov/2019058591
LC ebook record available at https://lccn.loc.gov/2019058592

ISBN 13: 978-1-03-223773-2 (pbk)
ISBN 13: 978-0-367-42359-9 (hbk)

Typeset in Times New Roman
by Apex CoVantage, LLC

This book is dedicated to my parents, Chris and Ian Robinson. Without their love and support, none of this would have been possible.

Contents

Figures

Tables

Boxes

Acknowledgements

There are many people to thank for their support while researching and developing this book, both in Morocco and at home in Sydney.

First, I would like to thank Professor Zoubida Charrouf (University of Rabat), Eric Defrenne (Yamana), Charlotte D'Erceville (BASF and LS), Rachel Ark (Cognis), Rachel Barre (L'Oréal) and particularly Latifa Anaouche for first showing me the argan forest, the women's cooperatives and for their openness with their argan business activities. I would like to very heartily thank all of the women who agreed to be interviewed in the cooperatives and for sharing their time, kindness and even a few meals! I would also like to thank my field assistants and translators Jamal Ouahi and Nadae Cherradi, as well as Eric Defrenne for helping with fieldwork. Thank you to Nadae and her family for doing additional follow-up research assistance for me in Morocco. Thank you to the High Commission for Forests and Water for meeting with us and explaining their forest management. Thanks also to Suhel Al-Janabi for updating me about the Moroccan ABS process and GIZ's work there.

In Australia, I would like to thank my wife Rachel and my children Miles and Felix for their patience and support. I would also like to thank my parents for lots of child-minding over the years! Thank you to anonymous reviewers who provided useful feedback on the manuscript and for some of my legal geography colleagues in Australia for providing some input, and Dr Jeffrey Nielsen who suggested some useful readings and ideas. Thanks to Professor Chris Gibson, who gave me lots of advice about this and other projects – it was too much for one or two papers, so here it is as a book! Thanks so much to Elizabeth (Lyb) Makin who read, edited, formatted and assisted with the final manuscript and for her excellent research assistance. Thank you to my former research assistants – most of whom have worked on other projects, but may have assisted at times with some of the work towards this.

Thank you to UNSW Science Faculty for supporting/funding this research, and also the Union for Ethical Biotrade (UEBT), particularly

Maria Julia Oliva, who invited me to Paris for the 'Beauty of Sourcing with Respect' conference in 2010, which started much of this activity and interest in argan on my part. Thank you to UNSW ethics for granting two approvals under which this research was undertaken. Thank you to the staff at the International Centre for Trade and Sustainable Development (ICTSD) in Geneva, for their advice and comments on this and other projects over the years – especially Pedro Roffe. Thanks also to the staff at Natural Justice, GIZ and ABS Initiative.

Thank you to Tim Hardwick, Hannah Ferguson, Amy Johnston, John Baddeley and others at Routledge – Taylor & Francis for their editing and support, and for getting the book published.

Last, I want to acknowledge that I am a white Anglo-Saxon man from Sydney, Australia, and it was my privilege to work with the cooperatives and to learn from the Amazigh women about argan and about their culture and lives. Any errors, misunderstandings or aspects 'lost in translation' I apologise for in advance. I hope this book inspires interest in the Amazigh people and their culture, and in the argan tree and forest. I also hope it inspires Amazigh women to tell their own stories and to record their culture and traditions for their own posterity.

1 Introduction

The argan tree and forest

Argania spinosa (*Argania spinosa (L) Skeels*, Sapotaceae) is a shrub or medium-height thermophilous (warmth-loving) tree with spiny branches and a characteristic snake-skin-like bark which, in favourable conditions, can live for 100 to 200 years (Charrouf and Guillaume, 2009; Ruas et al., 2011). The argan tree is endemic to Morocco and provides important ecological functions, with its deep root systems allowing for survival and stabilisation of soils in the arid and semi-arid ecosystems of the Souss-Massa-Drâa region (often called the Souss Valley) of southwest Morocco, the Anti-Atlas Mountains and surrounds bordering the Sahara Desert (see Figure 1.1). The tree survives in this region from the coast, inland to the mountains, across an area of approximately 950,000 hectares (le Polain de Waroux and Lambin, 2012) up to an altitude of 1,500 metres above sea level. From the Souss plain where the largest city in the region is found – Agadir – until the Anti-Atlas range, the annual rainfall varies between 150 and 250mm, up to 400 to 600mm in the Atlas Mountains (Ruas et al., 2011). Highly adapted to the arid conditions, tree growth slows or stops in times of low rainfall and the tree can reputedly remain dormant for up to ten years without water, re-foliating itself when precipitation returns (Ransley and Kamar, 2013). In the Souss region, the dominant endemic species is the argan tree, from valleys to hills and mountain slopes, often in poor soil conditions and in climatic extremes such as temperatures that can come close to 50 degrees Celsius. The argan tree might also be thought of as an important keystone species, serving as a foundation species that supports the ecology of over 1,200 plant and animal species, including 140 endemic species (Aymerich and Tarrier, 2010; UNESCO, 2019). With growing interest in the oil and intensifying land uses in the region, there are also cyclical and escalating pressures on the argan tree, which threatens the broader biodiversity of the Acacia–Argania ecoregion (Lybbert et al., 2011).

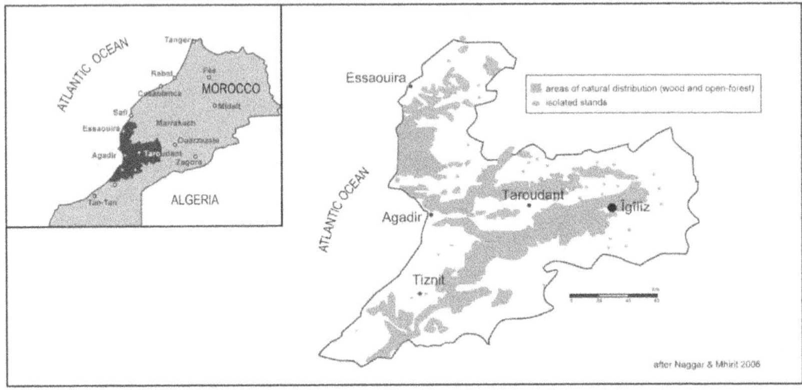

Figure 1.1 Map of the argan forest region and (a) the region as shown within Morocco

Source: Ruas et al., 2011, p. 428. Used with permission.

The argan tree (see Figure 1.2) is reportedly an 80-million-year-old relic tree species that has been known since the time of the Phoenicians, who established trade routes along the Mediterranean as far as the Moroccan coast around 600 BC (Charrouf and Guillaume, 2009). It is believed that during the Quaternary glaciations, the distribution of argan trees across Northern Africa reduced to the Souss Valley region of Morocco, where there were optimal conditions for its survival (Charrouf and Guillaume, 2009). Due to its relative isolation, it remains a regionally important biome which is increasingly threatened by human activities. Human land-use activities have impacted the forest for approximately the last 1,300 years, particularly through overgrazing by sheep and goats (McGregor et al., 2009; Ruas et al., 2011) and also for use of the wood for fires and charcoal (Khallouki et al., 2017), with anticipated acceleration of impacts from climate change (Lybbert et al., 2011).

Argan oil is extracted from the nuts of the argan tree, and the oil has been used traditionally by the Amazigh (also known as Imazighen or Berber peoples) as an alimentary oil, for skin care and as a cure for various ailments for at least nine centuries (le Polain de Waroux and Lambin, 2013). According to the texts of al-Bakri, a geographer and historian from Moorish Spain (d. 1094), the extraction of the oil followed the same procedure that applies today (Rocher, 1926, cited by Ruas et al., 2011). The Islamic doctor Abdullah Ibn Al-Baytar also drew attention to the tree and uses of the oil in his comprehensive treatise written in 1219, 'Kitab-al-Jami fil Adwiyah

Figure 1.2 A large argan tree being grazed by goats, near Taroudant

Source: Taken by the author, Daniel Robinson, 4 August 2010.

al-Mufradah' ('Dictionary of Simple Remedies and Foods') (Ransley and Kamar, 2013). For the Amazigh peoples of the region, the argan forest continues to provide an important livelihood source and income through the sale of argan oil for culinary, cosmetic and medicinal purposes, firewood and charcoal for heating and cooking, and food and shade for livestock (especially goats) (Lybbert et al., 2002).

Traditionally, the production of argan oil has been exclusively an Amazigh women's activity. Evidence of the use of argan from archaeological excavations in the region, and from texts from the 11th century, suggest that Amazigh women have been cracking argan nuts and using millstones to produce the oil since that time (Ruas et al., 2011). For most of this period, this would have been largely for domestic production and use by women, their families and local communities in the valley, and the collection of argan fruit remains a family activity to this day. But women have controlled the process of oil production – and this appears to have been due to prevailing gender roles, as the oil is used with cooking and for skin care or cosmetics purposes. However, it is important to highlight that Amazigh peoples often had matriarchal traditions and women were often revered as queens, warriors and goddesses (Symons, 2016). Berber households were often ruled by the wife or mother or the eldest woman, in contrast to typical Islamic households where there is a male head (Brett and Fentress, 1997, p. 242). Centuries of Islamic influence, and the colonial and early post-colonial eras have often had a suppressing impact on the rights and roles of women, until some advancement on equality since the late 1990s under reforms from King Mohamad VI (Maddy-Weitzman, 2011, p. 154). As Maddy-Weitzman explains: 'liberal forces, including Berber culture associations, were greatly encouraged by the king's actions on the issues of women's and human rights, for they corresponded to their own visions of a more pluralist and open society' (2011, p. 155).

The argan tree has created many jobs through the creation of women's cooperatives and, as such, these jobs have been marketed by companies and the cooperatives themselves as 'women's empowerment' activities. Women who previously would have had no source of formal income, but who would have undertaken household labour such as child-raising, farming and domestic duties, are now earning modest incomes by local standards. As Professor Zoubida Charrouf from the University of Rabat (one of the pioneers of the argan industry, argan research and argan cooperatives) explains, some women earn up to US$250 per month now, plus bonuses that are paid at the end of each year under fair trade or other arrangements in the cooperatives (Moulds, 2015). With newfound financial independence, women are able to choose how to spend their earnings, changing the status of women in the family, according to Charrouf: 'Women regain the capacity to decide, to manage their income and to invest in the future by sending their children [daughters especially] to school' (quoted in Moulds, 2015). This has arguably brought about a shift in the perception of women (both externally and within the cooperatives), particularly Amazigh women, who had been living much more 'domestic' lives until the expansion of the argan trade, as I will discuss in the following chapters. This is also occurring against the backdrop of a broader movement for Amazigh/Berber rights and women's rights in general, in the face of concerns arising about the effects of political Islam (e.g. polygamy and child marriage), Arab elitism, patriarchal conservatism limiting livelihood opportunities and schooling for women, and reported impunity for perpetrators of domestic violence (Salime, 2005; Symons, 2016).

Due to global interest in argan oil, the number of women's cooperatives is proliferating. Market demand for argan oil globally has rapidly expanded, with extensive international interest in uses of the oil for a range of skin- and hair-care products based on the oil and in some cases other components derived from the argan tree. The global argan oil market was 4835.5 tonnes in 2014 and is expected to reach 19,622.5 tonnes by 2022, which would put its market value at around US$1.79 billion (Khallouki et al., 2017). While this has undoubtedly brought some economic benefits to local producers, it is worth also investigating the role of these women in the value chain to these global markets, and the potential impacts of this growth in production on the argan forest itself. I will turn to some of these issues in the following chapters.

In recognition of its ecological value and the socio-economic importance of the argan forest, the region was declared a United Nations Educational, Scientific and Cultural Organization (UNESCO) Arganeraie Biosphere Reserve in 1998. This designation of more than 2.5 million hectares of forest area for the biosphere reserve is intended to enhance conservation efforts, as well as research, and support the socio-economic environment of the tree (UNESCO, 2002; Huang, 2017). Alongside this designation was a successful nomination and registration on the Representative List of the Intangible Cultural Heritage of Humanity for the 'argan environment, practices and know-how concerning the argan tree' in 2014 (Huang, 2017). This nomination specifically highlights the role of Amazigh women and their traditional methods for extracting the oil, their use of the oil, the pharmacopoeia and the crafting of tools used. The UNESCO nomination spanned four intangible cultural heritage domains: oral traditions and expressions, knowledge and practices concerning nature, traditional craftsmanship and 'other' aspects of cultural heritage (UNESCO, 2014; Huang, 2017).

Although endemic to Morocco, interest in the argan tree for commercial (and possibly ecological) benefits from the tree has seen other countries obtain cultivars of the tree. In the last half century, the argan tree has been introduced as a cultivated species in the deserts of Tunisia, Israel, Mexico and South Africa, among other parts of the world (Nouaim and Chaussod, 1993). While it is common that there is trade in plant biological resources and these have been grown in other regions, the distinctness of the species as a remnant in Morocco, and the traditional uses and knowledge of the Amazigh people, raise additional questions about appropriation. Given that multinational companies are now using, branding and marketing Moroccan argan oil products with various names and identities that draw upon or evoke its 'exotic' origins from the deserts of Morocco and from the Amazigh women, it is important to question what benefits these women receive and what implications there are for those on the producer end of the value and supply chains or networks.

Disciplinary underpinnings and structure of the book

The aim of this book is to make the reader think about the distinctness and uniqueness of the argan tree, the argan oil and the Amazigh producers who have used it for some 1,000 years or possibly more. As a product, argan oil is now often found in our hair-care products and face or skin creams, in bathrooms and supermarkets for consumers half a world away; it is marketed in evocative ways and this marketing draws upon a distant exoticism surrounding its origins. And yet it is produced by real people with real daily joys and struggles, who have a rich history but with many colonial and external influences, and in real environments with competing pressures for land and resource uses, and threats from commerce, other species and climate change. As the products travel, they take up new spaces in the imagination of the consumers who are not only consuming a product for care of their bodies, but also on some level the consumption of the exoticism of the product's origins.

For example, the global chain 'The Body Shop' markets products under the name 'Wild Argan Oil'. If we consider the term 'wild', its use often implies 'wilderness', which generally means remote places untouched by humans or with little human interference. Argan products are thus sold internationally with evocative language about distant exotic places, and ancient forests on the fringe of the Sahara and Atlas Mountains, as produced according to long-standing traditions by Berber women. In response to these trends, this book aims to understand the lives of these producers and the effects on the forest more deeply. Following the work of Head, Atchison and Gates (2012) on human-plant (bio)geographies (see also Head and Atchison, 2009), parts of this book consider how fundamental the argan plants/trees are in human lives, how humans have shaped the identity of the argan tree and argan oil in many ways over the centuries, but also how the argan tree has shaped the lives and identities of Morocco and its peoples – especially Amazigh women. Chapter 2 particularly follows these human–plant geographies and the bio-cultural importance of the argan forest in Amazigh lives and livelihoods.

The analysis and narration of this book draws upon a number of research approaches or fields within human geography, a toolkit of geographical approaches, including:

- geographies of following;
- production networks/value chains/geographies of making;
- legal geography; and
- human–plant (bio)geographies.

In thinking about the way argan is used, how it changes when it travels and how it is used in different countries and contexts, I draw first on a set of ideas and concerns from what has been called 'geographies of following' literature, which began as a concept led by Ian Cook and his 'follow the stuff' ethnography of everyday foods and consumer products from the source to the store and consumer (Cook, 2004; Cook et al., 2006; Cook and Harrison, 2007; Cook et al., 2017). As Cook explains, the research responds to David Harvey's (1990, p, 418) appeal to geographers to 'get behind the veil, the fetishism of the market' to make 'powerful, important, disturbing connections between Western consumers and the distant strangers whose contributions to their lives were invisible, unnoticed and largely unappreciated' (see also Cook, 2004; Cook et al., 2017). Cook's approach is highly ethnographic and multi-sited and describes the stories of multiple actors in the trade network or commodity chain of a specific product such as the humble papaya fruit (Chapter 5 in this book is close to this approach, drawing on Daya, 2014). He uses the following proposition:

> . . . if we accept that geographical knowledges through which commodity systems are imagined and acted upon from within are fragmentary, multiple, contradictory, inconsistent and, often, downright hypocritical, then the power of a text which deals with these knowledges comes not from smoothing them out, but through juxtaposing and montaging them . . . so that audiences can work their ways through them and, along the way, inject and make their own critical knowledges out of them.
>
> (Cook and Crang, 1996, p. 41; see also Cook et al., 2017)

This stream of work seeks to reconnect the lives of producers and consumers, but not through the linear commodity chain research that was common in the 1980s and 1990s (most prominently, in Gereffi and Korzeniewicz, 1994), but rather through the messy connections in the networks and systems behind commodity production, in engaged and also entangled research, underpinned by forms of radical politics (Cook et al., 2007).

Cook et al. (2007) themselves explain that the audience can find the messiness of their approach challenging, multi-sited, and deeply ethnographic. For this study on Moroccan argan, while keen to 'get behind the veil', my interest is also in understanding some of the underlying injustices, inequities or issues faced particularly by those people at the producer end of the commodity network, and the legal/regulatory, market-based and other influences which might cause or reduce these sorts of injustices. To some extent (particularly in Chapter 4), the research is influenced by the global production network (GPN) literature that aims to show the 'continuing unevenness of the spatiality of production and consumption, the differentiating role of structural and institutional conditions at various scales, and the responses and strategies of firms, non-firm organisations, and government bodies shaping the global economy over space and time' (Hess and Yeung, 2006). The GPN literature adopts a more qualitative and spatialised/networked approach to its precursor in the global value (and commodity) chain literature, in part recognising the messiness and entanglement that the 'following' literature undertakes; however, the GPN framework is arguably less radical, more structured and typically less intimate/larger scale. The interrelated GPN and global value chain (GVC) approaches explain geographical patterns of value creation, retention and capture in the global economy through descriptions of chain governance and network dynamics (Neilson et al., 2014). While an approach like this might be useful for political economic analysis of larger-scale commodities/products and for understanding structural and market forces, it does not quite have the nuance and complexity that is desirable for understanding the impacts upon the lives of local argan producers and what le Polain de Waroux and Lambin (2013, p. 590) describe as 'biological resource-based niche commodities'. This book therefore follows a hybrid approach that adopts some elements of GPN/GVC literature in Chapter 4, but then turns to more intimate approaches influenced by Daya's (2014) approach, which is focused on 're-imagining Southern producers in commodity stories', as well as those of Carr and Gibson (2016) and their 'geographies of making' in Chapter 5. These latter approaches focus more on the social life of making material goods, less from an economic or developmental perspective, but more in terms of what it means for those producers to apply their craft and skills. Carr and Gibson (2016) provoke us to consider the implications of a situation where crafting and handmaking cultures grow beyond immediate use value, towards a commercial imperative. As Dawkins (2010, p. 261) suggests, 'pleasure and self-fulfillment are often exchanged for what might otherwise be felt to be unstable, precarious, and even exploitive work' (see also Luckman, 2012). This consideration is of direct relevance to our thinking about the Amazigh women, whose ancestors have produced argan oil for centuries, to now analyse the effects and changes as commercial imperatives increase.

The book is also influenced by my interest in legal geography. This field is about understanding the interactions among law, space, place, scale and nature, and the socio-legal manifestations of these interactions (what Delaney, 2010, describes as the 'nomosphere'). Legal geography compels us to consider that in the 'world of lived social relations and experience, aspects of the social that are analytically identified as either legal or spatial are conjoined and co-constituted' (Braverman et al., 2014, p. 1). Connecting the diverse works that underpin the legal geographical endeavour, and distinguishing this field, is its 'fine-grained, detailed attention to the complex processes of legal constitutivity and a desire to understand the reciprocal or mutual constitutivity of the legal and the spatial' (Delaney, 2015, p. 98). The legal geography field then is used to disrupt ideas about the 'closure' of law as a discreet, formalistic or even archaic set of institutions (statutes, courtrooms, case law, contracts, etc.); it highlights the political nature, social relations and power relations of law-making and law enforcement (Blomley, 1994; O'Donnell et al., 2020). As a legal geographer, I am also interested in the way laws are created and transported, and the way they influence and impact on social and natural worlds, trade networks, and the co-constitution of laws and space/natures in this Moroccan case study. In the case of argan, there are the existing customary laws of the Amazigh people which have been overlain with state laws, as well as the influence of the UNESCO biosphere reserve designation. In addition, there have been concerns about the appropriation and patenting of plant biological resources of the argan tree by some companies, as well as other forms of intellectual property claims. Chapter 3 examines some of these issues, the responses of some companies through corporate social responsibility activities, and the potential for the Nagoya Protocol on Access to Genetic Resources and the Fair and Equitable Sharing of Benefits Arising from their Utilization to the Convention on Biological Diversity (2010) (hereafter, Nagoya Protocol) to provide an 'access and benefit-sharing' framework for the fair and equitable sharing of benefits relating to utilisation (through research and development – R&D) of the biological resources and their derivatives, as well as Amazigh traditional knowledge.

Methods, approaches and positionality/reflexivity

This book is based on both literature review and fieldwork in Morocco on four occasions, each for approximately two weeks – in August 2010, April and December 2011, and September 2014, plus follow-up correspondence with key contacts in 2017 and 2019. It is also informed by meetings with L'Oréal, Cognis (now BASF – a chemical company) and Yamana (a social responsibility non-governmental organisation – NGO) in December 2011 (with subsequent correspondence) and from discussions at the Union for Ethical BioTrade (UEBT) conference with the cosmetic industry in May 2011 (see Robinson and Defrenne, 2011), and in subsequent years.

Fieldwork in the Souss-Massa-Drâa Valley/region of Southern Morocco largely involved a combination of semi-structured one-to-one and focus-group-style interviews, as well as micro-ethnographic observations. The interviews were mostly focused on argan oil-producing cooperatives, as well as several interviews at seven businesses (selling and producing argan) and one association involved in the argan industry (also selling and producing). Interviews were conducted at the six cooperatives of the Economic Interest Group (EIG) Targanine, as well as at another EIG – L'Union des Coopératives des Femmes pour la production et la commercialisation de l'huile d'Argane (UCFA), at four cooperative locations. The total number of independent argan cooperatives interviewed was 14, and a further six argan businesses, shops or 'associations' were interviewed. The interviews were all translated by Moroccan field assistants in the local communities, who could speak Tamazigh and/or Arabic. These were focused on the region surrounding the city of Agadir, north to Imsouane and Tamanar, southeast to Ait Baha, and East to Tioute and surrounding areas near Taroudant. The women at the cooperatives were informed of the intent of the research and a witnessed prior verbal consent was obtained as required by relevant university human research ethics protocols, with some participants requiring us to maintain their anonymity. Reflexive research practice was undertaken, where there were follow-up discussions with the translators and EIG managers reflecting upon the research process, the responses from the women and the research approach.

As a non-Indigenous Australian male author, I began this work looking at Moroccan argan oil in the context of work globally for the protection of Indigenous knowledge – more specifically, in the context of the Convention on Biological Diversity (1992) and its emphasis on 'fair and equitable sharing of benefits arising from the utilisation of genetic resources' (and associated traditional knowledge). I recognise that my upbringing is seemingly worlds apart from the context of Amazigh women producing argan oil in the remote, arid Souss Valley of Morocco. It was within the context of 15 years' work on traditional knowledge and biodiversity that I undertook this work, and in doing so I acknowledge the potential socio-cultural gaps in my knowledge about the Amazigh production of argan. While this book cannot hope to explain every single thing about the Moroccan argan trade, it attempts to pull together much of the existing written academic material about the topic, supported by the additional insights and observations of several years of fieldwork. I hope the book encourages Amazigh women to tell their own stories about the argan tree and forest, and about their unique cultural heritage.

References

Aymerich, M. and Tarrier, M. (2010). *Un Désert Plein de Vie (Carnets de Voyages Naturalistes au Maroc Saharien, La Croisee de Chemins, Morocco)*. Casablanca, Morocco: Crossroads Press.

Blomley, N. (1994). *Law, Space, and the Geographies of Power*. New York and London: Guilford Press.

Braverman, I. (2014). Who's Afraid of Methodology? Advocating a Methodological Turn in Legal Geography. In I. Braverman, N. Blomley, D. Delaney and A. Kedar (eds). *The Expanding Spaces of Law: A Timely Legal Geography* (pp. 120–141). Redwood City, California: Stanford University Press.

Brett, M. and Fentress, E. (1997). *The Berbers*. The Peoples of Africa Series. Oxford: Blackwell.

Carr, C. and Gibson, C. (2016). Geographies of Making: Rethinking Materials and Skills for Volatile Futures. *Progress in Human Geography*, 40(3), pp. 297–315.

Charrouf, Z. and Guillaume, D. (2009). Sustainable Development in Northern Africa: The Argan Forest Case. *Sustainability*, 1(4), pp. 1012–1022.

Convention on Biological Diversity (1992), <https://www.cbd.int/>.

Cook, I. and Crang, P. (1996). The World on a Plate: Culinary Culture, Displacement and Geographical Knowledges. *Journal of Material Culture*, 1(2), pp. 131–153.

Cook, I. (2004). Follow the Thing: Papaya. *Antipode*, 36(4), pp. 642–664.

Cook, I. et al. (2006). Geographies of Food: Following. *Progress in Human Geography*, 30(5), pp. 655–666.

Cook I., Evans, J., Griffiths, H., Morris, R. and Wrathmell, S. (2007). 'It's More than Just What It Is': Defetishising Commodities, Expanding Fields, Mobilising Change. *Geoforum*, 38(6), pp. 1113–1126.

Cook, I. and Harrison, M. (2007). Follow the Thing: West Indian Hot Pepper Sauce. *Space and Culture*, 10(1), pp. 40–63.

Cook, I. et al. (2017). From 'Follow the Thing: Papaya' to followthethings.com. *Journal of Consumer Ethics*, 1(1), pp. 22–29.

Dawkins, N. (2010). Do-it-yourself: The Precarious Work and Postfeminist Politics of Handmaking (in) Detroit. *Utopian Studies*, 22(2), pp. 261–284.

Daya, S. (2014). Beyond Exploitation/Empowerment: Re-imagining Southern Producers in Commodity Stories. *Social & Cultural Geography*, 15(7), pp. 812–833.

Delaney, D. (2010). *The Spatial, the Legal and the Pragmatics of World-making: Nomospheric Investigations*. Oxon: Routledge.

Delaney, D. (2015). Legal Geography I: Constitutivities, Complexities, and Contingencies. *Progress in Human Geography*, 39(1), pp. 96–102.

Gereffi, G. and Korzeniewicz, M. (eds) (1994). *Commodity Chains and Global Capitalism*. Westport, Connecticut: Praeger.

Harvey, D. (1990). Between Space and Time: Reflections on the Geographical Imagination. *Annals of the Association of American Geographers*, 80(3), pp. 418–434.

Head, L. and Atchison, J. (2009). Cultural Ecology: Emerging Human–Plant Geographies. *Progress in Human Geography*, 33(2), pp. 236–245.

Head, L., Atchison, J. and Gates, A. (2012). *Ingrained: A Human Bio-Geography of Wheat*. Burlington: Ashgate.

Hess, M. and Yeung, H. (2006). Whither Global Production Networks in Economic Geography? Past, Present, and Future. *Environment and Planning A*, 38(7), pp. 1193–1204.

Huang, P. (2017). Liquid Gold: Berber Women and the Argan Oil Co-operatives in Morocco. *International Journal of Intangible Heritage*, 12(1), pp. 140–155.

Khallouki, F., Eddouks, M., Mourad, A., Breuer, A. and Owen, R. (2017). Ethnobotanic, Ethnopharmacologic Aspects and New Phytochemical Insights into Moroccan Argan Fruits. *International Journal of Molecular Sciences*, 18(11), pp. 2277–2301.

Le Polain De Waroux, Y. and Lambin, E. F. (2012). Monitoring Degradation in Arid and Semi-Arid Forests and Woodlands: The Case of the Argan Woodlands (Morocco). *Applied Geography*, 32(2), pp. 777–786.

le Polain De Waroux, Y. and Lambin, E. F. (2013). Niche Commodities and Rural Poverty Alleviation: Contextualizing the Contribution of Argan Oil to Rural Livelihoods in Morocco. *Annals of the Association of American Geographers*, 103(3), pp. 589–607.

Luckman, S. (2012). Precarious Labour Then and Now: The British Arts and Crafts Movement and the Ethics of Rural Cultural Work Re-visited. In S. Luckman (ed.). *Locating Cultural Work: The Politics and Poetics of Rural, Regional and Remote Creativity* (pp. 48–84). Basingstoke: Palgrave Macmillan.

Lybbert, T., Aboudrare, A., Chaloud, D., Magnan, N. and Nash, M. (2011). Booming Markets for Moroccan Argan Oil Appear to Benefit Some Rural Households While Threatening the Endemic Argan Forest. *Proceedings of the National Academy of Sciences*, 108(34), pp. 13963–13968.

Lybbert, T., Barrett, C. and Narjisse, H. (2002). Market-Based Conservation and Local Benefits: The Case of Argan Oil in Morocco. *Ecological Economics*, 41(1), pp. 125–144.

Maddy-Weitzman, B. (2011). *The Berber Identity Movement and the Challenge to North African States*. Houston: University of Texas Press.

McGregor, H. V., Dupont, L., Stuut, J. B. W. and Kuhlmann, H. (2009). Vegetation Change, Goats, and Religion: A 2000-year History of Land use in Southern Morocco. *Quaternary Science Reviews*, 28(15–16), pp. 1434–1448.

Moulds, J. (2015, 29 April). Argan Oil: The Cost of the Beauty Industry's Latest Wonder Ingredient. *The Guardian*, <https://www.theguardian.com/sustainable-business/2015/apr/28/argan-oil-beauty-anti-ageing-loreal-lush-berber>.

Nagoya Protocol on Access to Genetic Resources and the Fair and Equitable Sharing of Benefits Arising from their Utilization to the Convention on Biological Diversity (2010), <https://www.cbd.int/abs/doc/protocol/nagoya-protocol-en.pdf>.

Neilson, J., Pritchard, B. and Yeung, H. (2014). Global Value Chains and Global Production Networks in the Changing International Political Economy: An Introduction. *Review of International Political Economy*, 21(1), pp. 1–8.

Nouaim, R. and Chaussod, R. (1993). L'Arganier: Argania Spinosa (L.) Skeels. (Sapotacées). *Le Flamboyant: Bulletin de Liaison des Membres du Réseau Arbres Tropicaux*; *Association Silva: Paris, France*, 27(1), pp. 7–9.

O'Donnell, T., Robinson, D. and Gillespie, J. (2020). Introduction: What's Different about the Australasian and Asia-Pacific Approach to Legal Geography? In T. O'Donnell, D. Robinson and J. Gillespie (eds). *Legal Geography: Perspectives and Methods* (pp. 3–16). Oxon: Routledge.

Ransley, A. and Kamar, A. (2013). *The Complete Book of Argan Oil*. Milton Keynes: Marvel Oils Books.

Robinson, D. and Defrenne, E. (2011). *Argan: A Case Study on ABS*. Amsterdam: Union for Ethical Biotrade.

Ruas, M.-P., Tengberg, M., Ettahiri, A., Fili, A. and Van Staëvel, J.-P. (2011). Archaeobotanical Research at the Medieval Fortified Site of Îgîlîz (Anti-Atlas, Morocco) with Particular Reference to the Exploitation of the Argan Tree. *Vegetation History and Archaeobotany*, 20(5), pp. 419–433.

Salime, Z. (2005). *Between Islam and Feminism: New Political Transformations and Movements in Morocco*. Chicago, Illinois: University of Illinois Press.

Symons, E.-K. (2016, 24 March). Morocco's Indigenous Amazigh Women Unite against Islamists and Arab Elites. *Women in the World*, <https://womenintheworld.com/2016/03/24/matriarchal-traditions-in-north-africa-under-threat-from-islamists-and-arab-elites/>.

UNESCO (2002). Biosphere Reserve Information: Morocco, Arganeraie, <http://www.unesco.org/mabdb/br/brdir/directory/biores.asp?code=MOR+01&mode=all>.

UNESCO (2014). Report on the Status of an Element Inscribed on the List of Intangible Cultural Heritage, <https://ich.unesco.org/en/RL/argan-practices-and-know-how-concerning-the-argan-tree-00955>.

UNESCO (2019). Strengthening of the Argan Biosphere Reserve (SABR), Morocco, <https://en.unesco.org/biosphere/arab-states/arganeraie>.

2 Human–plant geographies and the biocultural significance of argan

The biocultural significance of argan

In a book about the argan tree and the unique Moroccan argan forest, it is important to reflect on our ideas about plants, nature, protected areas and 'wilderness'. The way in which we perceive and frame nature and natural areas or landscapes is important, because it can define and influence the way we then might 'manage', govern or protect that landscape. Particularly for Indigenous peoples, but also for the environments which they have customarily inhabited and in which they have interacted with nature, it is important to recognise their role in shaping and sustainably using ecosystems and biodiversity (Hill et al., 2011). As Castree (2013) explains, for decades, the subject of 'nature' was left to zoologists, botanists, chemists and 'physical scientists', but increasingly, in recent decades, nature has become the remit of the social scientist – particularly geographers who traditionally straddle the human–physical divide. In part, this is due to the recognition that humans are certainly part of nature (we are animals) and always have been. But, in recent decades, recognition that humans have been dramatically altering and impacting upon the environment in alarming ways has led to a range of concerns about population growth, industrialisation, urbanisation and consumption (see e.g. *The Limits to Growth* by Meadows et al., 1972; and *Our Common Future (The Brundtland Report)* by the World Commission on Environment and Development, 1987). A reactionary response to this has been to separate humans from nature, almost unconsciously, in an effort to 'preserve' or isolate existing valuable ecosystems. For example, national parks and protected areas are often established to protect threatened habitat, endangered species of plants and animals, ecological remnants or sometimes migratory species.

While the in-situ protection of these species and ecological communities is critical, it has sometimes been undertaken in colonial and oppressive ways for Indigenous peoples and local communities. Indeed, in some cases, subsistence farmers or 'peasants', economically poor local people and Indigenous peoples have been easy targets to blame for incidents of environmental degradation through cash cropping or informal mining (see e.g. Forsyth and Walker, 2008; Fisher et al., 2012) that often have their causes in distant locations and markets, where the demand for goods arises. This thinking still continues today, and ideas of 'wilderness' are prevalent in some parts of the population, as well as more active ideas and efforts for 're-wilding' or 're-naturing' (Rotherham, 2014). But at least in the academic sphere, a binary between nature and culture, or humans (us here) and environment (out there), has gradually been criticised and debunked (see e.g. Castree and Braun, 2001; Whatmore, 2002).

In response, and in recognition of the livelihoods and roles of Indigenous peoples and local communities, there have been efforts to highlight the cultural and spiritual values of biodiversity (e.g. Posey, 1999), and the customary and sustainable use of ecosystems and natural resources by these populations. There is now a significant amount of literature on 'biocultural diversity' which started through the United Nations Environment Program's (UNEP) mapping of the links among biological, cultural and linguistic diversity globally (Maffi and Woodley, 2010). According to Maffi (2007, p. 269), '[b]iocultural diversity comprises the diversity of life in all its manifestations – biological, cultural and linguistic – which are interrelated (and likely co-evolved) within a complex socio-ecological adaptive system'. In practice, biodiversity conservation depends on and derives from long-term, predictable, sustainable, traditional or customary land uses. A loss of cultural heritage may result when traditional land-use systems decline or end, and this can also be associated with a reduction in flora and fauna biodiversity (Agnoletti and Rotherham, 2015; Amici et al., 2015). Because long-term, predictable human activities have transformed environments, biocultural landscapes under traditional or customary management frequently hold the most significant and diverse ecological resources (Agnoletti and Rotherham, 2015).

The importance of the argan trees and forest to Amazigh lives and livelihoods is through a biocultural association. Following approaches such as Head, Atchison and Gates' (2012) work on human-plant (bio)geographies (see also Atchison and Head, 2012), we consider how fundamental the argan plants/trees are in human lives, and how humans have shaped the growth and identity of the argan tree and argan oil in many ways over the centuries, but also how the argan tree has shaped the lives and identities of Morocco and its peoples – especially the Amazigh women. As noted in Chapter 1, argan oil has been used by the Amazigh for hundreds, if not thousands, of years as a food oil and as a skin- or hair-care product (Charrouf and Guillaume, 2009). The first written record known to exist regarding these uses is from the 11th century, followed by reports by the famous physician Ibn Al Baytar in 1219 (Charrouf, interview, 4 August 2010; Khallouki et al., 2017). The uniqueness and significance of the arid argan landscape, when linked to the long-standing traditions of argan oil production and cultural heritage, arguably demonstrates a unique *terroir* or character of the plants and oil, which in turn is being used to market and protect the oil as belonging to this distinct biocultural landscape (see Chapter 3).

Ingold (2000) argues for a relational approach to understanding people's lived experience of inhabiting landscapes, with both cultural knowledge and bodily substance undergoing continuous generation in the ongoing engagement between land and beings – human and non-human. As Ingold (2000) explains, the work of a farmer or herder (or in this case sometimes an argan nut harvester) is not to *make* crops or livestock, but rather to set up conditions of development within which plants and animals take on particular forms of behavioural disposition and processes of *growth*. The plants might be nurtured, utilised, harvested, used as fodder or propagated, or they might be damaged or destroyed. Further than this, Ingold (2010) argues that there may be cultural and spiritual connections to land and 'nature', such as plants. Recent excavations in the Souss Valley region suggest that, since the 11th century, the argan tree was cultivated by the Amazigh as a source of wood for construction, fodder for livestock and an edible oil (Ruas et al., 2011). Throughout recent history, ethnobotanical and economic botany texts indicate that the 'rural people' (presumably predominantly Amazigh people) in the Souss Valley region remained dependent on the argan seed for oil, with the argan tree described as critical to their livelihoods and existence (Morton and Voss, 1987). Streets (1962) indicates that 'both foliage and fruit are very palatable to cattle, sheep and goats', and the young shoots, although spiny, 'form almost the only forage available at some periods of the year' (see Figure 2.1) (Githens and Wood, 1943, cited in Morton and Voss, 1987, p. 227). Goats, which have historically been herded widely throughout the region and still are currently, have been sustained by the argan tree and have been a vital source of milk, meat and hide for human populations for centuries (see Figure 2.2) (Morton and Voss, 1987, p. 227). In economic terms, nearly 90 percent of the rural economy of the region has depended on argan-based agroforestry in recent decades (Benchekroun, 1990), and this is likely to have been the case for a much longer period.

Figure 2.1 Close-up of branches and fruit of an argan tree
Source: Taken by the author, Daniel Robinson, 4 August 2010.

Figure 2.2 Goats eating the upper fruits of an argan tree
Source: Taken by the author, Daniel Robinson, 1 May 2011.

Human–plant geographies and the argan craft

An Institut de recherche pour le développement (IRD) research program, 'Politiques publiques et gestions paysannes de l'arbre et de la foret: alliance durable ou dialogue de dupes?' (POPULAR) has highlighted that agricultural and arboricultural practices have shaped the growth of the tree over long periods of time. They have observed in the argan forest the ruins of earthworks such as terraces, channels and levelled areas, which were formerly cultivated fields (IRD, 2011). The team argue that preparation of the ground, as well as forms of domestication, have been applied to the argan tree – and that this is a generally poorly recognised evidence of ancestral Amazigh *savoir-faire*. Local people have selected and cultivated shoots to regenerate the forest stand, as well as pruning, lopping and cleaning trees of dead and diseased wood to enhance tree growth (IRD, 2011). They explain that these techniques enhance and encourage growth according to its intended uses for grazing, fruit harvesting, side hedges or firewood (IRD, 2011). Most other articles and reports note that the argan tree typically defies domestication (see e.g. UNESCO, 2019), but it seems as though there is evidence of ancient through to modern human–argan interactions (see also Ruas et al., 2011).

The production of argan oil has traditionally been entirely a women's activity, and it is believed that this has been the case for hundreds of years or since the first uses of the oil. Amazigh women have traditionally collected the fallen ripe fruit with their families, sun-dried the fruit, and then removed the pulp and peel. Traditionally, the argan nuts are broken with flat stones of a specific size and weight and the kernels are then air-dried in clay containers and roasted by mild heating (field observations, 2010–14). Roasted kernels are cooled and then ground into a brownish dough or paste by hand using millstones. To extract the oil, the paste is hand-pressed until it hardens, and the obtained brown emulsion is decanted – thus furnishing a transparent oil with a hazelnut-like taste. The extracted residue, or 'pressed cake' as it is often described, is dark brown and generally still contains up to 10 percent oil (Charrouf and Guillaume, 1998; field observations, 2010–14). This pressed cake is a by-product that is often fed to goats, cattle and livestock, or it can be used as a useful argan-oil-containing exfoliant in soap (see Figure 2.3).

The latter part of the process has since been mechanised, but women are still typically the ones involved in cracking the argan nuts prior to pressing the kernels for oil (Huang, 2017). The process of cracking the argan nuts is quite specialised, and the Amazigh women perform this task with expertise. The cracking of the nut is an important tactile skill developed through haptic perception and learning, which I explain further below. Carefully selected

Figure 2.3 From bottom to top: argan fruit, nuts, shell, almond, pressed cake, and bread

Source: Taken by the author, Daniel Robinson, 30 April 2011.

flat stones are chosen for their appropriate weight (not too heavy and not too light) and shape in order to break to argan nuts. Ingold (2000; 2010) invites us to think about the tool as being more than a mere mechanical adjunct to the body, serving to deliver a set of commands issued to it by the mind; rather, it extends the whole person. It is used not to control, but to reveal. Ingold (2000, p. 319) elaborates as follows:

> Indeed there is a certain parallel between the use of tools in production and the giving and receiving of gifts in exchange. The tool has an impact on raw material, as the gift has an impact on its recipient, only so long as it is animated by an *intention* that issues from the person of the user or the donor . . . Both tool and gift mediate an active, purposive engagement between persons and their environments.
>
> [emphasis in the original]

The stone/tool chosen is important and this choice relies upon the haptic perception and skill of the Amazigh women. If the argan nut inside shatters, then it will oxidise and produce poor quality oil (see Figure 2.4). The

Figure 2.4 Women cracking argan nuts with stone on plinth or brick at a cooperative

Source: Taken by the author, Daniel Robinson, 1 May 2011.

women gradually develop an understanding of the force required to carefully crack the nut without splitting the inner kernel. This appears to have been the case for centuries, with documents in the 11th century describing the extraction of the oil, which is the same procedure that applies today (Rocher, 1926, cited by Ruas et al., 2011). Gibson (1966, p. 123) described the haptic system as '[t]he sensibility of the individual to the world adjacent to his[/her] body by use of his body'. Gibson (1966, drawing from Weber, 1851) emphasised the close link between haptic perception and body movement, and that haptic perception is active sensory and physical exploration. This corporeal interaction among human, object and plant is significant to the ongoing production of quality (unoxidised) oil, and therefore to the livelihoods of the region and the whole regional economy.

This sort of material production remains persistently central to life throughout the world and, certainly, to production (and then consumption), as demonstrated through the 'geographies of following' literature noted in Chapter 1. But through industrialisation and modernisation, the embodied tasks of manual labour were typecast as repetitive and even demeaning, while the mind tasks became associated with higher levels of education, skill, economic value and intellectual satisfaction (Carr and Gibson, 2016). Unfortunately, what is often being lost is an appreciation of the artisanal craft and skill involved in what may often be seen as manual labour or 'basic tasks'. Carr and Gibson (2016) argue for recognition of a full spectrum of 'making cultures', along with the sensibilities and dispositions that are centred on a deep and considered relationship with materials. This thinking can certainly be extended to the deployment of technical skills with plants like argan, where there is a mutually constitutive interrelation between human and non-humans (Ingold, 2000; Head, Atchison and Gates, 2012).

Gradual mechanisation of the traditional craft

Many women have formed or joined cooperatives and, as is described in the following chapters, the volume of oil produced has dramatically risen and the economic importance of argan has soared. The oil of pressed argan kernels is now known to be high in vitamin E, carotenes and essential fatty acids, making it ideal for use in skin- and hair-care products, and driving international demand (Charrouf and Guillaume, 1998). But the distribution of those benefits from the argan trade has varied significantly (Lybbert et al., 2010; Lybbert et al., 2011; le Polain de Waroux and Lambin, 2013). The role of women has recently started to change in some areas and some 'cooperatives' or businesses have been encroached upon partially or almost entirely by men as the value of argan oil has increased. This gender shift and the marketisation of argan oil has undoubtedly shifted the situated social experience of argan production. As Hoffman (2008) explains, the term *tamazirt* is used in different ways by different people to represent rural places (and land), such as the argan groves of the Souss Valley. In recent decades, as men have left these regions for cities, the burden of hard rural labour in the *tamazirt* has increasingly fallen on women to look after crops such as barley. But the rise of global interest in argan oil has shifted this relationship somewhat, and interviews showed that men are increasingly interested and involved in argan 'cooperatives', even if the companies marketing argan oil and products are continually marketing the 'women's empowerment' aspects of their production process.

The mechanisation of parts of the oil production process has also increased and, as foreign interest and demand has increased for the oil, so has both its export value and the level of organisation of the cooperatives (often with the support of European development assistance or aid agencies). For at least two decades now, mechanical presses have been used in cooperatives and businesses to extract argan oil from the kernels. This allows a simplified procedure, and no mixing of the paste and water, with a much quicker extraction process of the oil from the kernels (Charrouf and Guillaume, 1998). However, it was reported during fieldwork in 2012 and 2014 that a new cracking technique had been developed and patented, and was being fine-tuned to increase the speed and volume of nuts that it could crack, as well as to avoid the splitting of the kernels (and the oxidisation of the oil). Cracking the nuts is the dominant mechanism for labour payment of the Amazigh women, alongside collection of the raw fruit and nuts by families. As Turner (2016) argues, the cracking machines weaken the position of the women as producers, who have previously been indispensable to the production of quality oil. With increased industrialisation comes time pressure, and refocused divisions of labour and task orientation – all of which alter the practice of these skills and situated social experiences or cultures of making (Ingold, 2010; Carr and Gibson, 2016). Sources in the region have argued that the mechanised cracking technology is still poor and continues to produce poor quality oil, so this has not become a dominant feature of the oil's production for many cooperatives (interviews and personal communication, 2014, 2019). Another way of looking at this, from a 'more-than-human' perspective (Whatmore, 2006; Panelli, 2010), is that the argan nut has embodied agency and is an important part of the control of this process. The associations between the Amazigh women and the argan trees and nuts are important to livelihoods in more detailed ways than can be realised at first glance, and produce a sense of 'humans as enmeshed with rather than outside non-human nature' (Head and Muir, 2006, p. 510; see generally Panelli, 2010).

Traditional cultural significance of argan

The continuation of 'traditional' practices of production, even if some are being mechanised, protects important facets of cultural heritage, which are also important for Amazigh women's identity and pride (interviews, see Chapter 5). The argan tree – often described as a relic tree, due to its longevity – may still retain for some Amazigh people a cultural significance that parallels the relic biophysical nature of the tree. As Brett and Fentress (1997) explain, despite the dominance of both Islam within Amazigh society for hundreds of years now and Arab cultural influence, there are a range of preceding Berber beliefs about magic and spirits throughout Morocco and adjoining countries. They highlight that there can be domestic spirits, which include the tutelary spirits of particular trees in the countryside, which are hung with white rags to mark a pact with the spirit (Brett and Fentress, 1997). These may often be argan trees, and some of these trees were noted during fieldwork in 2014. However, people did not seem to want to be interviewed about or to discuss this practice in detail, potentially due to potential contradictions with dominant Arab-Islamic beliefs or judgement from peers. As Hoffman (2006, p. 144) explains, there was cultural-linguistic Amazigh-Tamazight suppression until the 1990s:

> Arabising tendencies in this multiethnic (Arab-Berber) part of the world began during the French Protectorate (1912–1956), as the archival records suggest. While classical Arabic is closely associated with Islam, the shared religion of Arabs and Berbers, there is no evidence demonstrating that Arabic's 'sacred' character . . . has spurred language shift in itself in Morocco. Instead, factors encouraging language shift away from Berber and towards Arabic include changes in political economies that put Tamazight ('Berber' language) speakers in wage labor positions with Arab supervisors and owners and the emergence of symbolic capital in the form of state diplomas as a gateway to economic betterment. Linguistic markets have consolidated and centralized around Arabic-dominant institutions, marginalizing the Tamazight indigenous language varieties. Massive (cultural) Arabization and (linguistic) Arabicization in the 1970s was coupled with widespread urbanization in a decade of drought.

The cultural significance of the argan tree to the Amazigh-Berber peoples is an important point for consideration given the legal and commodification aspects of the rapidly expanding argan trade. Indeed, Amazigh activism and local rights have actively perpetuated and presented a coherent representation of an endangered cultural unity, drawing on early Berber studies and depicting a somewhat more mythical 'time before state national time', which probably blurs the history and diversity of the Amazigh peoples and their cultures (Silverstein, 2010, p. 83). Notwithstanding this, there have been rights struggles and attempts at 'retribalization of the village space' in order to retain control over resources, as well as cultural and linguistic domains (Hoffman, 2010; Silverstein, 2010, p. 90). As discussed below, there have been significant moves towards recognition of this cultural heritage, as well as challenges for the protection of the forest.

Impacts and protections for the argan forest

Despite the increasing commercial value of the oil and its significance to the Amazigh people, the tree has not always been highly valued – particularly by the French colonial powers and also by other land users. The distribution of the forest has been in decline for centuries, particularly over the last century. By the year 1900, it is reported that 150,000 to 200,000 hectares had disappeared, as population pressure spread southwards through Morocco (Morton and Voss, 1987). During World War I, demand for wood accelerated, particularly shipments to Spain, and French property owners destroyed trees while clearing for agricultural purposes. By 1924, the Moroccan Forest Service had restricted annual charcoal production to between 52,000 and 80,000 tonnes and recommended the use of other trees in order to save the argan tree, with legislation eventually enacted to reduce felling of argan trees (Morton and Voss, 1987). However, this felling reportedly continued in World War II with demand for timber to export to France serving as a major contributor to the reduction of the argan forest from around Essaouira in Central Morocco, further south towards the Souss Valley and Agadir (Morton and Voss, 1987). Some of these historical texts blame 'local people' for the felling, but Amazigh people met in the field generally refuted this, particularly in the modern context, as they have always had customary rules surrounding the use and protection of the tree. For most Amazigh interviewees, they noted that some local people would collect fallen branches for charcoal or firewood in winter and suggested that some people might be collecting too much Argan fruit or even shaking, hitting or breaking branches to make more fruit fall. But in interviews at the cooperatives and argan businesses, blame for loss of forest coverage was often directed towards clearing for other agricultural purposes by wealthy landowners, and camel herders who reputedly drive camels up from the Western Sahara, Mauritania or Algeria, and who were often described as 'Touareg/Tuareg' (nomadic), as distinct from Amazigh Berber peoples (interviews, 2012, 2014). The other issue, which people would only reluctantly comment on, was the impact of goat herding, which was seen as a lesser issue to camel herding in interviews around Imsouane and the road north to Essaouira (interviews, 2014).

Interview responses generally concurred with the findings of Lybbert, Magnan and Aboudrare (2010; see also Lybbert, Barrett and Narjisse, 2004). Amazigh families that had benefited from the argan boom had newfound income, and often did not know how to spend it (Targanine interviews, 2012). Women said that they would sometimes share the money with their husbands – and this was often put towards farming, including goat herding (interviews, UCFA, Targanine, other cooperatives, 2012, 2014). Lybbert, Magnan and Aboudrare (2010) argue that adding goats to a household's herd generally benefits the household (more milk, meat and hides), but harms the forest. As awareness has grown, locals are now less likely to let their goats browse in the tree canopy or will limit browsing to non-harvest seasons (interviews, 2011, 2012). However, goats still regularly climb and browse trees outside the fruit harvest season and so continue to place pressure on the forest. During fieldwork, I also witnessed goat grazing within the harvest season in areas near Taroudannt (see Figures 1.2 and 2.2). Lybbert, Magnan and Aboudrare (2010) suggest that changes in local practices and attitudes are becoming motivated more by immediate concerns about the fruit harvest than by longer-term concerns for tree productivity or forest sustainability. They argue that locals have changed the way in which they use the forest to increase their personal fruit harvest, and rising argan prices have not necessarily turned them into champions of the forest's future. At most of the cooperatives visited, there was an acknowledgment of people damaging the forest, but many argued that their cooperative members were well trained and instructed not to damage the forest, and that there were fines and penalties from the High Commissariat on Water, Forests, and Combating Desertification for damage to trees (interviews, 2011, 2012, 2014).

In a separate paper, Lybbert and colleaugues (2011) also use satellite data to assess landscape-level trends in the density of the argan forest and forest canopy. By comparing these trends before and after the onset of the argan boom in 1999, they show a number of trends of largely forest decline in the modelled satellite images. Before the boom, negative trends prevailed in some portions of the southern argan forest because of the dramatic expansion of irrigated agriculture in that region during the 1980s and 1990s (Lybbert et al., 2011), which interviews (2010, 2011) suggest had occurred in the southern part of the region. Since the boom began, much of the northern argan forest appears to have also thinned. It is likely that the northern forest has attracted greater attention during the boom because of its proximity to major markets and popularity among tourists (close to the popular walled city of Essaouira and coastal surfing/wind-surfing towns), and this pattern seems consistent with the boom's negative impacts upon this part of the forest (Lybbert et al., 2011). Some of the cooperatives in the northern region were also the ones which expressed the greatest concern about the struggle and challenges to produce and market argan oil (interviews, 2014). Indeed, during fieldwork in the northern region, the argan forest appeared noticeably thinner than in areas close to Agadir and inland from Agadir – where greater protections have been focused and where the UNESCO Biosphere Reserve is located.

In recognition of its ecological value and the socio-economic importance of the argan forest, the region was declared as the Arganeraie UNESCO Biosphere Reserve in 1998. The core area of this designation comprises the Souss-Massa National Park. This designation of more than 2.5 million hectares of sclerophyllous forest area for the biosphere reserve is intended to enhance conservation efforts, as well as research, and to support the socio-economic environment of the tree (UNESCO, 2002; Huang, 2017). Alongside this declaration was a successful nomination for, and subsequent registration on, the Representative List of the Intangible Cultural Heritage of Humanity for the 'argan environment, practices and know-how concerning the argan tree' in 2014 (Huang, 2017). This listing specifically highlights the role of Amazigh women and their traditional methods for extracting the oil, their use of the oil, the pharmacopoeia and the crafting of tools used, and they span four intangible cultural heritage domains: oral traditions and expressions, knowledge and practice concerning nature, traditional craftsmanship and 'other' aspects of cultural heritage (UNESCO, 2014; Huang, 2017). UNESCO (2019) reporting on the forest highlights that despite it becoming the world's most expensive edible oil (approximately US$300 per litre), there are mixed benefits for the forest and women and this situation needs to be improved. The report further notes that argan oil cooperatives have been supported by NGOs and domestic and international development agencies, and that 'these partners have made all efforts that the increase in export price actually trickles down to local people and that it preserves the health of the argan forest, through a win-win constellation' (UNESCO, 2019). Perhaps also relying on Lybbert (2011) and his team's analyses, UNESCO (2019, p. 1) argues that the argan boom has:

> . . . enabled rural families to increase consumption and investment, in particular to increase their goat herds – yet with negative effects on the argan forest. At the same time, families can send their girls to secondary school, so educational outcomes, especially for girls, have improved greatly. In addition, the increased return on female labour might improve women's position in intra-household bargaining.

In addition to the Biosphere Reserve declaration, there are reforestation programs occurring across different land-use types. Turner (2016, p. 399) is critical of some of these programs because they have used molecular research to optimise the argan tree, which he sees as a 'shift from the inherent biodiversity of natural argan woodlands to species standardisation and ultimately privately owned tree plantations following a different normative logic'. Alongside shifts in the forestry legislation, this change in property regimes relevant to the argan resource is arguably a 'dramatic shift in the nomosphere' (Turner, 2016, p. 399) or the legal geography of the argan forest, which will be explored in more detail in Chapter 3.

References

Agnoletti, M. and Rotherham, I. (2015). Landscape and Biocultural Diversity. *Biodiversity and Conservation*, 24(13), pp. 3155–3165.

Amici, V., Landi, S., Frascaroli, F., Rocchini, D., Santi, E. and Chiarucci, A. (2015). Anthropogenic Drivers of Plant Diversity: Perspective on Land Use Change in a Dynamic Cultural Landscape. *Biodiversity Conservation*, 24(13), pp. 3185–3199.

Atchison, J. and Head, L. (2012). Yam Landscapes: The Biogeography and Social Life of Australian 'Dioscorea'. *Artefact: The Journal of the Archaeological and Anthropological Society of Victoria*, 35(1), pp. 59–74.

Benchekroun, F. (1990, October). Un systeme typique d'agroforesterie au Maroc: L'arganeraie. Séminaire Maghrébin d'Agroforesterie, Jebel Oust, Tunisie.

Brett, M. and Fentress, E. (1997). *The Berbers*. The Peoples of Africa Series. Oxford: Blackwell.

Carr, C. and Gibson, C. (2016). Geographies of Making: Rethinking Materials and Skills for Volatile Futures. *Progress in Human Geography*, 40(3), pp. 297–315.

Castree, N. (2013). *Making Sense of Nature*. London: Routledge.

Castree, N. and Braun, B. (eds) (2001). *Social Nature: Theory, Practice, and Politics*. Malden, Massachusetts and Oxford: Blackwell.

Charrouf, Z. and Guillaume, D. (1998). Ethnoeconomical, Ethnomedical, and Phytochemical Study of Argania Spinosa (L.) Skeels: A Review. *Journal of Ethnopharmacology*, 61(7), pp. 7–14.

Charrouf, Z. and Guillaume, D. (2009). Sustainable Development in Northern Africa: The Argan Forest Case. *Sustainability*, 1(4), pp. 1012–1022.

Fisher, R., Maginnis, S., Jackson, W., Barrow, E. and Jeanrenaud, S. (2012). *Linking Conservation and Poverty Reduction: Landscapes, People and Power*. London: Routledge.

Forsyth, T. and Walker, A. (2008). *Forest Guardians, Forest Destroyers: The Politics of Environmental Knowledge in Northern Thailand*. Chiang Mai: University of Washington Press and Silkworm Books.

Gibson, J. (1966). *The Senses Considered as Perceptual Systems*. Boston, Massachusetts: Houghton Mifflin.

Githens, T. S. and Wood, C. E., Jr. (1943). *The Food Resources of Africa*. African Handbooks 3. Philadelphia, Pennsylvania: University of Pennsylvania Press.

Head, L., Atchison, J. and Gates, A. (2012). *Ingrained: A Human Bio-Geography of Wheat*. Burlington: Ashgate.

Head, L. and Muir, P. (2006). Suburban Life and the Boundaries of Nature: Resilience and Rupture in Australian Backyard Gardens. *Transactions of the Institute of British Geographers*, 31(4), pp. 505–524.

Hill, R., Cullen-Unsworth, L., Talbot, L. and McIntyre-Tamwoy, S. (2011). Empowering Indigenous Peoples' Biocultural Diversity through World Heritage Cultural Landscapes: A Case Study from the Australian Humid Tropical Forests. *International Journal of Heritage Studies*, 17(6), pp. 571–591.

Hoffman, K. (2006). Berber Language Ideologies, Maintenance, and Contraction: Gendered Variation in the Indigenous Margins of Morocco. *Language & Communication*, 26(2), pp. 144–167.

Hoffman, K. (2008). *We Share Walls: Language, Land and Gender in Berber Morocco*. Oxford: Blackwell.

Hoffman, K. (2010). Internal Fractures in the Berber–Arab Distinction: From Colonial Practice to Post-National Preoccupations. In K. Hoffman and S. Miller (eds). *Berbers and Others: Beyond Tribe and Nation in the Maghrib* (pp. 39–62). Bloomington, Indiana: Indiana University Press.

Huang, P. (2017). Liquid Gold: Berber Women and the Argan Oil Co-operatives in Morocco. *International Journal of Intangible Heritage*, 12(1), pp. 140–155.

Ingold, T. (2000). *The Perception of the Environment: Essays on Livelihood, Dwelling and Skill*. London: Routledge.

Ingold, T. (2010). The Textility of Making. *Cambridge Journal of Economics*, 34(1), pp. 91–102.

Institut de recherche pour le développement (IRD) (2011). The Moroccan Arganeraie Shaped by Human Endeavour. IRD Scientific Newssheets, no. 367, <http://www.en.ird.fr/the-media-centre>, accessed 12 December 2019.

Khallouki, F., Eddouks, M., Mourad, A., Breuer, A. and Owen, R. (2017). Ethnobotanic, Ethnopharmacologic Aspects and New Phytochemical Insights into Moroccan Argan Fruits. *International Journal of Molecular Sciences*, 18(11), pp. 2277–2301.

le Polain De Waroux, Y. and Lambin, E. F. (2013). Niche Commodities and Rural Poverty Alleviation: Contextualizing the Contribution of Argan Oil to Rural Livelihoods in Morocco. *Annals of the Association of American Geographers*, 103(3), 589–607.

Lybbert, T., Aboudrare, A., Chaloud, D., Magnan, N. and Nash, M. (2011). Booming Markets for Moroccan Argan Oil Appear to Benefit Some Rural Households While Threatening the Endemic Argan Forest. *Proceedings of the National Academy of Sciences*, 108(34), pp. 13963–13968.

Lybbert, T., Barrett, C. and Narjisse, H. (2004). Does Resource Commercialization Induce Local Conservation? A Cautionary Tale from Southwestern Morocco. *Society & Natural Resources*, 17(5), pp. 413–430.

Lybbert, T., Magnan, N. and Aboudrare, A. (2010). Household and Local Forest Impacts of Morocco's Argan Oil Bonanza. *Environment and Development Economics*, 15(4), pp. 439–464.

Maffi, L. (2007). Biocultural Diversity and Sustainability. In J. Pretty, A. S. Ball, T. Benton, J. Guivant, D. R. Lee, D. Orr, M. J. Pfeffer and H. Ward (eds). *The SAGE Handbook of Environment and Society* (pp. 267–277). London: SAGE.

Maffi, L. and Woodley, E. (2010). *Biocultural Diversity Conservation: A Global Sourcebook*. London: Earthscan.

Meadows, D. H., Meadows, D. L., Randers, J. and Behrens, W. W. (1972). *The Limits to Growth*. Washington, DC: Potomac Associates.

Morton, J. and Voss, G. (1987). The Argan Tree (Argania Sideroxylon, Sapotaceae), A Desert Source of Edible Oil. *Economic Botany*, 41(2), pp. 221–233.

Panelli, R. (2010). More-than-human Social Geographies: Posthuman and Other Possibilities. *Progress in Human Geography*, 34(1), pp. 79–87.

Posey, D. A. (UNEP) (1999). *Cultural and Spiritual Values of Biodiversity*. London: Intermediate Technology and UNEP.

Rotherham, I. (2014). The Call of the Wild: Perceptions, History, People & Ecology in the Emerging Paradigms of Wilding. *ECOS*, 35(1), pp. 35–43.

Ruas, M.-P., Tengberg, M., Ettahiri, A., Fili, A. and Van Staëvel, J.-P. (2011). Archaeobotanical Research at the Medieval Fortified Site of Îgîlîz (Anti-Atlas, Morocco) with Particular Reference to the Exploitation of the Argan Tree. *Vegetation History and Archaeobotany*, 20(5), pp. 419–433.

Silverstein, P. (2010). The Local Dimensions of Transnational Berberism: Racial Politics, Land Rights, and Cultural Activism in Southeastern Morocco. In K. Hoffman and S. Miller (eds). *Berbers and Others: Beyond Tribe and Nation in the Maghrib* (pp. 3–62). Bloomington, Indiana: Indiana University Press.

Streets, R. (1962). *Exotic Forest Trees in the British Commonwealth*. Oxford: Clarenden Press.

Turner, B. (2016). Supply-Chain Legal Pluralism: Normativity as Constitutive of Chain Infrastructure in the Moroccan Argan Oil Supply Chain. *Journal of Legal Pluralism and Unofficial Law*, 48(3), pp. 378–414.

UNESCO (2002). Biosphere Reserve Information: Morocco, Arganeraie, <http://www.unesco.org/mabdb/br/brdir/directory/biores.asp?code=MOR+01&mode=all>.

UNESCO (2014). Report on the Status of an Element Inscribed on the List of Intangible Cultural Heritage, <https://ich.unesco.org/en/RL/argan-practices-and-know-how-concerning-the-argan-tree-00955>.

UNESCO (2019). Strengthening of the Argan Biosphere Reserve (SABR), Morocco. UNESCO Man and the Biosphere Programme Website, <https://en.unesco.org/biosphere/arab-states/arganeraie>.

Weber, E. (1851). *The Doctrine of the Sense of Touch and Common Sense Founded on Experiments*. Brunswick: Friedrich Vieweg und Sohn.

Whatmore, S. (2002). *Hybrid Geographies: Natures Cultures Spaces*. London: SAGE.

Whatmore, S. (2006). Materialist Returns: Practising Cultural Geography in and for a More-than-human World. *Cultural Geographies*, 13(4), pp. 600–609.

World Commission on Environment and Development (1987). *Our Common Future (The Brundtland Report)*, <https://sustainabledevelopment.un.org/content/documents/5987our-common-future.pdf>.

3 Legal geographies of argan

Scales of nature and knowledge regulation

Introduction to legal geography

Legal geography has developed as a field of study over recent decades, gaining increasing recognition for its role in providing a critical forum for analysis of law–space–society relations. Although there are antecedents in kin disciplines of critical legal studies, law and society, and legal anthropology (see e.g. von Benda-Beckmann et al., 2009; Davies, 2017), legal geography has been drawing its own lines on the scholarly map for some time now (see O'Donnell et al., 2020). Nicholas Blomley's (1994) *Law, Space and the Geographies of Power* was probably the original defining piece of scholarship that brought together the concept of legal geography/geographies. Blomley (1994, p. 51) explains that these critical geographies 'seek to reconstruct the law-space nexus so as to accord proper recognition to both and to affirm the complex interplay of the two, evaluating the manner in which legal practice serves to produce space yet, in turn, is shaped by a sociospatial context'. Legal practitioners have arguably presented law as abstract, immaterial and universal, and as a 'closed' specialist system, perpetuating the mythology of equal representation, objectivity and blind justice (Braverman, 2017; see also Blomley, 1994). Law is also constructed as anthropocentric terrain, with nature and space rendered as either legal subject or mere object, to be defined and ruled (Delaney, 2003). Critiquing these ideas, legal geographers like Braverman (2014, p. 1) compel us to consider that in the 'world of lived social relations and experience, aspects of the social that are analytically identified as either legal or spatial are conjoined and co-constituted'.

A recent succession of papers (Bartel et al., 2013; Bennett and Layard, 2015; Delaney, 2015; 2016) have explained and reviewed the development of this field since its emergence in the mid-1990s (see especially Blomley, 1994). The field is characterised by a diversity of work that focuses on the relationships among laws, spaces, places, scales, natures and territories.

Legal geographers have highlighted many ways in which peoples, places, cultural and environmental contexts intersect and have important influence over the way in which laws operate, and their reflexive effect on those contexts (Bartel and Graham, 2016; Gillespie, 2016; O'Donnell, 2016; Robinson and Graham, 2018). Connecting the diverse works that underpin the legal geographical endeavour, and indeed distinguishing this field, is its 'fine-grained, detailed attention to the complex processes of legal constitutivity and a desire to understand the reciprocal or mutual constitutivity of the legal and the spatial' (Delaney, 2015, p. 98).

As explored in a recent special issue on legal geography and legal pluralism (Robinson and Graham, 2018), jurisdiction, or scales of law, operate at local, nation-state and international levels and, importantly, also between these levels, such that 'one cannot speak of law and legality but rather of interlaw and interlegality' (Santos, 1987, p. 288). Legal pluralism refers to the situation where 'in any one geographical space defined by the conventional boundaries of a nation state, there is more than one "law" or "legal system"' (Davies, 2012, p. 805). This is probably an under-reported phenomenon, given the colonial history of many countries around the world and the reluctance of many states to acknowledge the customary laws of Indigenous peoples (Tobin, 2014). This is probably partially true of Morocco, where Amazigh customs relating to argan trees are being recognised in the context of their conservation, but where there are undoubtedly still land-use conflicts (Turner, 2014; 2017). In addition, because of the operation and enforcement of multiple laws and regulations on place from multiple scales in specific places, those places may have competing or resistant social norms, customs or material conditions that impact upon the 'closure' and effectiveness of laws. Indeed, there are often geopolitical impositions of international laws from 'above' – not just through colonialism, but through more normative diplomatic and political-economic processes (Robinson, 2013; Robinson and Graham, 2018). Over two decades ago, Santos (1987, p. 288) wrote that 'socio-legal life is constituted by different legal spaces operating simultaneously on different scales and from different interpretive standpoints'. The construction of different legal orders through which the same social objects are regulated (Santos, 1987; 2002; see also Proulx, 2005) foreshadows Delaney's (2010, p. 71) 'nomospheric traces', which follow the performance of multiple strands of the legal/nomic in 'worldly' contexts or social spatialities. These analyses help us to spatially contextualise the mutual constitution of multiple laws, places and subjects (both human and non-human) and to unpack these through particular case studies or local spatial conflicts (Robinson and Graham, 2018).

Using these legal geography approaches, I aim to analyse first the land-use laws and challenges in relation to the argan tree and argan oil production. Second, I reflect upon international biodiversity laws, including the Convention on Biological Diversity and the Nagoya Protocol to consider the way in which they respond to challenges relating to the protection of Indigenous knowledge, and the potential appropriation of that knowledge within the dominant intellectual property regime. Last, I continue this thinking about intellectual property, marketing and branding in the context of naming conflicts over 'Moroccan Argan Oil' and the resulting attempts to protect the geographical origins of argan oil.

Law, space and land

There are customary usufruct rules surrounding the use of the argan tree on different land tenure types. This affects goat grazing, along with where and when people can harvest argan. Although these rules have been in place for generations, there has been exploitation of the forest for charcoal and firewood, building materials and grazing for animals (goats and camels), as well as collection of the fruit (which may potentially affect propagation if overzealous). As a result, the Moroccan Haut Commissariat aux Eaux et Forêts et à la Lutte Contre la Désertification (High Commissariat on Water, Forests and Combating Desertification) has established laws in the local region to control and minimise damage to the argan forest, and in support of the formal UNESCO Biosphere Reserve designation (see Chapter 2).

In interviews, the effectiveness of these approaches vis-à-vis the existing customary laws was discussed. Before delving into these interviews, however, it is important to first recognise that Amazigh customary rules have existed for use of the argan forest for potentially hundreds of years. While some argan trees can be found on private land, most households access argan fruit via seasonal usufruct rights in defined forest tracts called *agdal*. During harvest season (May to September), other uses are restricted (see Figure 3.1). Once the fruit harvest is over, the usufruct tracts of land return to collective use. Other portions of the forest, called *azroug*, are collectively exploited year-round by members of the local village (Lybbert et al., 2004). This process has been observed as a customary practice for generations. As one Targanine cooperative manager (interview, 2014) put it: 'They [the women] know the customary rules and know the land areas where they can collect, like they know their own children.'

From 1917 onwards, under protectorate conditions of the French colonial government in Morocco, all forest areas were declared the domain of the state, and national legislation regulating the use of the forest in Morocco was enacted (Turner, 2014). Special legislation was adopted for

Figure 3.1 Private compounds in the foreground and agdal land with argan forest in the far background, near Cooperative Taitmatine, Tioute

Source: Taken by the author, Daniel Robinson, 4 August 2010.

the *Arganeraie*, which allowed for more extensive access by local people than for other forest areas, and also for recognition of usufruct rights (Turner, 2014).

This was then followed by the designation of part of the region as the *Arganeraie* UNESCO Biosphere Reserve, as already noted in Chapter 2. A Forestry Code was specifically developed for the *Arganeraie* based on earlier Moroccan forest laws (Aubert et al., 2009)[1] and related strategies and programs for implementation of the *Arganeraie* were designed with the traditional uses of the argan forest by Amazigh people in mind, and generally reflect the customary rules for use of the forest, albeit with stricter punishments for damaging trees and with state enforcement of the rules (High Commissariat, 2019). The Arganeraie Biosphere Reserve covers an area of 2.5 million hectares, across the provinces and prefectures of Agadir Ida Outanane, Ait Melloul Inzeguane, Chtouka Ait Baha, Taroudant, Tiznit and Essaouira (see Figure 3.2). Under the Biosphere

Reserve, there are a number of zones for co-management of the forest, as follows:

- 18 core areas (A zones) covering 16,620 hectares. Their delineation took into consideration: (i) the ecological context related to the presence of the argan tree and difficult access/steep terrain; (ii) the existence of significant and interesting natural phenomena, such as the presence of a settlement well away from argan trees, rare animals or plant species; and (iii) the absence of human activities (houses, tracks, etc).
- 13 buffer zones (B zones) covering 582,450 hectares. Inclusion within these zones was based on the following criteria: (i) existence and importance of the argan tree (scattered or low-density stands are excluded, areas at risk of erosion are included); and (ii) importance of the argan tree in the local economy.
- 14 transition zones (development zones or C zones) that encompass areas not covered by zones A and B. The objective assigned to these zones is the achievement of sustainable socio-economic development of the area of the *Arganeraie* (High Commissariat, 2019).

Figure 3.2 Argan fruit drying outside a Targanine cooperative – the hill behind is covered in argan trees

Source: Taken by the author, Daniel Robinson, 30 April 2011.

The High Commissariat has programmed a number of measures at each biosphere reserve area (zones A, B and C), as part of integrated conservation and development strategies of the entire area. These measures have a duration of 20 years with priority programs/activities implemented over the first five years, as follows:

- At the level of the protection zones (A): (i) establish a protocol of agreement of protection with the population (system of compensation of the rights of use, system of repurchase of these rights, system of exchange land, etc.); (ii) develop the inventory and intervention program; (iii) set up an observatory for zones A and B; and (iv) deepen scientific research.
- At the level of buffer zones (B): (i) support integrated rural development; (ii) fight against erosion, especially water erosion; (iii) carry out forest management plans; (iv) promote vocational training; (v) rationalise pastoral exploitation; (vi) promote the marketing of local products; (vii) promote the self-organisation of the population; and (viii) encourage the substitution and saving of fuelwood.
- At the level of the transition zones (C): (i) encourage the conservation and protection of the environment; (ii) involve investors and lowland farmers in the conservation of the argan ecosystems; and (iii) involve NGOs in the area of promoting local products and protecting the *Arganeraie*.
- Accompanying measures at the level of all zones: in parallel with the specific measures for each of the zones, the following additional measures, across all zones A, B and C, are necessary: (i) promote environmental education; (ii) ensure the sustainability of the argan ecosystem through natural or assisted regeneration; (iii) achieve reforestation with multiple uses; (iv) enhance the value of agricultural production systems; (v) reforest multiple uses; and (vi) promote extra-forestry activities (e.g. beekeeping, artisanal fisheries, small-scale farming) (High Commissariat, 2019).

Forestry agents and local Amazigh inhabitants sometimes enter into an authority-based relationship and agree on protocols for the protection of the forest and its use in specific areas. But, occasionally, it has been reported that local people have sometimes avoided this and symbolically re-appropriated their forest, often by performing rituals to sacralise the boundary markers set by spirit wardens (IRD, 2011). The Amazigh-state relationship with regard to the argan forest thus appears to have occasional ongoing tensions. It is both interesting and important to recognise that some trees and forest areas have been recognised locally as sacred, and also that the Amazigh have maintained their customary practices, rules and laws for argan trees amidst the influence of state and supra-state influences, such as the UNESCO regime.

In addition, the influence of market demand and the high value of the oil has created a temptation to overharvest fruit either from areas where harvesting might normally be banned, or by over-vigorous collection techniques (e.g. striking or breaking branches). In interviews, it was noted by cooperative members that, despite good knowledge of the laws and rules, and the threat of large fines from the High Commissariat, some people still damaged the trees or collected from places where they should not (interviews, 2012, 2014). More than once while walking in the surrounds of a cooperative or travelling to a cooperative cracking centre, I saw goats browsing lower tree branches. The goat herders were scolded by the cooperative managers, and they then quickly moved their goats away (fieldwork, 2012, 2014).

In response to the gradual degradation of the argan forest, discussed in Chapter 2, there have been a number of NGO, aid agency and other attempts to replant tracts of forest. These reforestation activities have occurred on a number of different land-use types, including private land. Turner (2016) is critical of some of these programs because they have used molecular research to seek to improve argan seeds with the intention of transforming argan into an optimised crop through the selection of genotypes exhibiting the desired properties of higher quality and greater quantity (Turner, 2016, citing Bellefontaine, 2010; ANDZOA/INRA, 2015). Turner (2016, p. 399) sees this as a 'shift from the inherent biodiversity of natural argan woodlands to species standardisation and ultimately privately-owned tree plantations following a different normative logic'. Alongside shifts in the forestry legislation, this change in the property regimes providing the argan resource is arguably a 'dramatic shift in the nomosphere' (Turner, 2016, p. 399) or the legal geography of the argan forest. While this shift was not described as being dramatic in our interviews with cooperatives and argan businesses (2012, 2014), a few people did note some land-use changes, and in one major supply chain it was noted that argan leaves were collected only from a private property (interviews, 2014). Indeed, as will be discussed further below, this was a legal requirement from the High Commissariat, that the leaves used in the L'Oréal supply chain, for one of their patented argan technologies used in a skin-care cream, be sourced from areas not covered by the Moroccan Forestry Code and not within the *Arganeraie*. Within the Biosphere Reserve, it is seen as important not to encourage any pruning of trees, even if just for the collection of leaves, since it may damage the trees and impact growth.

Law, nature and science/knowledge

In addition to the expansion of argan market demand from local and tourist populations, the international export market has rapidly grown. As Lybbert (2007, p. 12) notes, 'introducing cosmetic argan oil into high value international markets has required research into both the chemical properties of the oil and potential extraction and processing technologies'. Although a significant amount of the preliminary biochemical research on argan was undertaken by Professor Zoubida Charrouf, a Moroccan researcher at the University of Rabat, this was taken further particularly by a number of European companies. As a result of their research, companies such as Cognis (now BASF) and L'Oréal have patented isolated active ingredients for skin-care products from argan trees. The practice of claiming intellectual property protection over specific innovations regarding plants, while often legal, raises a range of ethical and socio-legal questions about the use and cultural significance of plants to different societal groups. In this case, both the long history of traditional use and Amazigh knowledge of the tree and thus the potential for it to have sacred significance – as revealed in a number of interviews where customary laws were discussed – highlight a number of potential injustices that arise relating to/out of assertions of intellectual property rights.

Since the late 1980s and early 1990s, there have been NGO and activist critiques about the 'biopiracy' of plant- and animal-based products and associated Indigenous or traditional knowledge. Different actors and interest groups have argued different sides of the debate surrounding bioprospecting or biodiscovery (Reid et al., 1993; Hayden, 2003). Prior to and during the negotiations which established the Convention on Biological Diversity (1992) at the United Nations Conference on Environment and Development (UNCED) – often referred to as the Rio Earth Summit – there were arguments about the potential win-win that bioprospecting could provide for conservation of resources, while also advancing scientific research and development (R&D). Aspects of this concept were enshrined in the Convention on Biological Diversity's text, including in article 1 (the objectives), which promotes 'the fair and equitable sharing of the benefits arising out of the utilization of genetic resources' (commonly described here as 'access and benefit-sharing' – ABS). In this context, the utilisation of resources refers to R&D. While, for some actors, this provided a potential funding mechanism for conservation, for others it was about ensuring equity in relation to the development of 'value-added' products based on resources and knowledge from developing countries and Indigenous peoples and local communities. Others were much more critical, arguing that the framing of the Convention on Biological Diversity in terms of 'sovereign rights over natural resources' would inevitably mean that Indigenous peoples and local communities would rarely be beneficiaries (Harry, 2011). The discourse of 'biopiracy' emerged (see Box 3.1 for a typology), as a critique of the use and expansion of intellectual property to cover genetic resources, and as a counter-discourse to intellectual property 'piracy' (e.g. the copying of copyright-protected films, CDs, DVDs).

Box 3.1 Typologies and categories of biopiracy

Patent-based biopiracy: The patenting of (often spurious) inventions based on biological resources and/or traditional knowledge that are extracted without adequate authorisation from other (usually developing) countries, indigenous or local communities.

Non-patent biopiracy: Other intellectual property control (through plant variety protection or deceptive trademarks) based on biological resources and/or traditional knowledge that has been extracted without adequate authorisation from other (usually developing) countries, indigenous or local communities.

Misappropriations: The unauthorised extraction of biological resources and/or traditional knowledge from other (usually developing) countries, Indigenous or local communities.

Source: Robinson (2010, p. 21).

Parallel to the Convention on Biological Diversity, there was a series of negotiations in relation to trade and intellectual property. Minimum standards and norms for intellectual property rights allowing patents over plant and animal products were something that started occurring in free trade agreements (mostly by the United States) in the 1980s, and were then argued into the text of the Marrakesh Agreement Establishing the World Trade Organization: Annex 1C Trade-Related Aspects of Intellectual Property Rights (1994) (TRIPS Agreement), which provides that:

> 27.3. Members may also exclude from patentability:
>
> (b) plants and animals other than micro-organisms, and essentially biological processes for the production of plants or animals other than non-biological and microbiological processes. However, Members shall provide for the protection of plant varieties either by patents or by an effective sui generis system or by any combination thereof . . .

This means that forms of intellectual property protection *must* be applied to plants and micro-organisms, but there is some very limited flexibility in how this is done. As a legal geographer, it is important to point out here that this resulted in the significant reshaping and globalisation of Euro-American legal norms in relation to intangible property claims over nature and living natural resources. Through technological advancements and the shifting of the normative framework for what would be allowed under patent and intellectual property claims, a number of industries (e.g. pharmaceuticals, biotechnologies, cosmetics, industrial enzymes, crop protection and agri-business) have thus been able to extend and protect their intellectual property portfolios globally, including in many countries which are now WTO members that would stand to benefit very little from such arrangements. Indeed, the African Group and other countries like Bolivia have since argued that patent claims over life forms are immoral and should be banned (see e.g. African Group, 2003). Despite this, the dominance of neoliberal capitalist norms has seen these minimum intellectual property standards normalised. Around the world, the standards for protection within intellectual property systems are probably rising due to the negotiation of free trade agreements as pursued by the most advanced economies, in what Drahos (2002) describes as the TRIPS-plus ratchet effect.

Moroccan argan oil was identified as one example of concern by NGOs in the report, *Out of Africa: Mysteries of Access and Benefit-Sharing* (McGown, 2006). Although it does not go as far as to call the Moroccan example 'biopiracy', there are related concerns and questions raised. The report highlights that, from late 2000 onwards, the Cognis Corporation had filed US and European patent applications relating to a number of their products, sold by their French subsidiary, Laboratoires Sérobiologiques. McGown (2006, p. 16) explains that Cognis was selling three argan products: Arganyl (leaf extracts), Argatensyl (fruit extracts) and Lipofructyl Argan (oil), using evocative terms to describe the 'ancestral beauty rituals' of the Amazigh women that were the inspiration for their products. McGown (2006, pp. 16–17) goes on to critique or question the activities and partnership:

> Cognis says it works in partnership with local groups, but I could not find documentation of a benefit-sharing agreement for Cognis' patent applications and sale of argan products. One article by Cognis authors claims that the company's argan products are 'fair trade'; but Cognis' idea of fair-trade sounds strange: '*The cooperatives agree to sell the fruit of their enterprises at market prices that ensure an adequate return to sustain their activity. Furthermore, from an economic point of view, they ensure that women receive a salary equivalent to the local minimum wage* . . .' Cognis says this arrangement is particularly helpful to women; but market prices that simply '*sustain their activity*' and a minimum wage don't sound out of the ordinary to me. If a benefit agreement that valorizes genetic resources or traditional knowledge

> exists, it may not be public. At any rate, I did not find it. In any case, there is substantial latitude to question whether the Cognis 'inventions' should be patentable at all because they very closely correlate with traditional uses of argan and it is unclear what patentable innovation the company has contributed. Although Moroccan communities may be receiving some benefit from Cognis – perhaps as minimum wage suppliers of raw material or perhaps more – it appears that Moroccan traditional knowledge has been claimed as the intellectual property of a German company.
>
> [emphases in the original]

However, when I came to contact and start reviewing the arrangements in place (later, in 2010–14) for the Moroccan argan oil value chains that relate to these products and patents, they were described in much more positive terms. Cognis (and its French cosmetics division Laboratoires Sérobiologiques – LS, both of which eventually became part of BASF), in partnership with L'Oréal, appears to have responded to McGown's critique, or they realised that, under the Convention on Biological Diversity and its subsequent Bonn Guidelines (2002), it would bring negative publicity if they did not establish a more substantial partnership with the cooperatives with whom they worked. The early marketing of the Laboratoires Sérobiologiques Argan Program in Morocco (2011), provided to me by Cognis staff, explains their efforts to ensure fair return, non-monetary benefits, protection of biodiversity, protection of traditional knowledge and local empowerment, much of which seems to pre-empt the concerns raised by McGown, and then to continue to respond to these early critiques.

The Targanine–Cognis–L'Oréal benefit-sharing arrangement

Having explored many biopiracy cases in my 2010 book *Confronting Biopiracy*, I was encouraged by one reviewer to do follow-up research on case studies to highlight the possibility of 'fair and equitable access and benefit-sharing agreements'. With this impetus, I contacted Cognis about their patents and corporate social responsibility (CSR) program for argan oil and argan products, which appeared to me, at least from their website description, to be something like a benefit-sharing agreement.

To provide some backstory of this specific argan supply chain and research activities, between 1994 and 2005, Professor Zoubida Charrouf helped a group of Amazigh women to establish the six cooperatives (Ajdigue, Tagmate, Tamaynoute, Targante, Toudarte and Taitmatine) that now operate under the economic interest group (EIG) and brand 'Targanine'. According to Professor Charrouf and the cooperative managers, these were established with the aim of benefiting and empowering local women for supply of argan oil and products to these burgeoning markets. These Targanine cooperatives, through their connections with Professor Charrouf, then entered into commercial agreements with Cognis (which was later acquired by German chemical giant, BASF) and subsequently L'Oréal that are of interest in the ABS context. In 2010, 2011 and 2014, these cooperatives were interviewed to understand the arrangements made for the supply of argan oil and the benefits that occurred as a result of the CSR agreement established.

It appeared that the traditional uses and knowledge of Amazigh women has prompted further investigation by researchers and companies for decades now, with significant research activity beginning in the 1980s with firms focusing on culinary oil, pure argan oil for cosmetic uses, and also R&D into extracts of bioactive ingredients from argan oil, leaves, fruit and seeds – this is where ABS is relevant (Lybbert, 2007). In this case, of particular interest is the research established as a partnership between Professor Zoubida Charrouf and Cognis around 2000, with patent applications occurring in the United States and Europe from 2001, and with patents granted in 2005, 2006, 2008 and 2011. These include:

- cosmetic and/or dermo-pharmaceutical preparations containing native proteins from the plant *Argania spinosa* (US Patent Number 7,871,766, granted on 18 January 2011, first filed on 28 November 2001);
- cosmetic and/or dermo-pharmaceutical preparations containing leaf extracts of the plant *Argania spinosa* (US Patent Number 7,105,184, granted 12 September 2006, first filed 28 November 2001);
- cosmetic and/or pharmaceutical preparations that contain an extract of the plant *Argania spinosa* (2000) (EP1276460 B1):

    - claim 1: a cosmetic and/or pharmaceutical preparation that contains saponins from an extract of the plant *Argania spinosa*;
    - claim 2: the preparation as claimed in claim 1, however characterised that the extract is obtained by extraction from parts of plants, selected from the group consisting of the leaves, the roots, the stem, the bark, the flowers, the fruits, the fruit flesh and the seeds.

- a plant extract and its pharmaceutical and cosmetic use (2003) (EP1711194 B1):

    - claim 1: the triterpene-fraction of the extract of the pulp of the fruit of *Argania spinosa*;
    - claim 2: the non-saponifiable-fraction of the extract of the pulp of the fruit of *Argania spinosa*.

L'Oréal has also filed several patent applications which note the use of argan oil as a potential ingredient in vegetable oils used for skin- or hair-care products. They also cite the use of BASF-branded extracts such as Arganyl[tm] (leaf extract) in some of their patented innovations. Notably, none of the patents appears to make claims over the oil or extracts from the oil (Robinson, 2014). This is likely due to the existing prior art and traditional knowledge of the oil for cosmetic purposes, and due to the need for 'inventiveness' or 'non-obviousness' as a patent criterion. It is likely that a biochemical extract from the oil, which is known to have cosmetic benefits, would be obvious to a dermatologist – someone 'skilled in the art/science'. Interestingly, the Cognis patents thus focus on proteins extracted from a by-product, and also flavonoids isolated from the leaf. Arguably, these are considerably more 'novel and inventive' biochemical isolations than if they had been focused on argan oil (Robinson, 2014). Through varied technological designs adapted from the genetic resource and its biochemical extracts, and due to the expanded regulatory protections offered by the now globalised intellectual property laws, new opportunities for (intangible/industrial) property claims emerge. The law-nature-knowledge nexus has been substantially disrupted and rewritten.

The development of the ABS process under the Convention on Biological Diversity was seen as a response to the threat of 'biopiracy' and has been intended to create the possibility of establishing a clearer framework whereby 'access' to a plant or animal (genetic resource) is only possible with 'prior informed consent' – which often means a government-issued permit, as well as local community or land-holder permissions. In addition, the ABS process is also supposed to provide for benefit-sharing to the providers of the plant or animal resources and associated traditional knowledge (for detailed information on the Nagoya Protocol, see Robinson, 2014; Morgera, Tsioumani and Buck 2014; Robinson and von Braun, 2019).

Because Morocco did not yet have a designated ABS law, there was not an explicit 'access' requirement in the country for the 'utilization of genetic resources'. During meetings with Cognis and L'Oréal staff, it was emphasised that the required legal permissions, such as phytosanitary certificates, had been obtained. Preliminary research was also conducted in-country by Professor Charrouf, who is named on a number of the patents as an inventor (Charrouf and Guillaume, 1999; Charrouf and Guillaume, 2009), prior to further R&D by BASF and L'Oréal towards a number of marketable skin- and hair-care products. Some of these products utilise commercial argan oil (not patented and outside of the scope of ABS), while others utilise the specific biochemical extracts derived from the argan tree that have been identified through R&D. These latter products would arguably be within the scope of the Convention on Biological Diversity and particularly the Nagoya Protocol concept of 'utilization of genetic resources' once it comes into force and is nationally implemented by countries (I return to the Nagoya Protocol later in this chapter). Because this R&D occurred without domestic ABS laws in Morocco, this case can then be considered an ABS hypothetical (Robinson, 2014).

Benefit sharing set-up

The tripartite partnership has been established since 2008 between BASF (formerly Cognis), L'Oréal and Yamana for the implementation of a CSR program along the supply chain for supply and use of argan products. The Targanine cooperatives in Morocco supply argan oil and related argan products (e.g. pressed oil cake and argan leaves) to BASF under fair-trade arrangements of prepayment for the product (two-year contract for the supply of oil), pre-agreed prices and a premium price paid (e.g. 5 percent premium paid for oil at the end of the year since 2010). BASF maintains elements of quality control and refinement of the raw products. L'Oréal is supplied with the refined product, which it then incorporates into a number of cosmetics and related skin- and hair-care products that are distributed internationally, making the whole partnership economically viable. Yamana (an NGO focused on social responsibility for products like textiles and cosmetics) has a key role as a trainer and facilitator working with the cooperatives in Morocco, ensuring that local stakeholder expectations are being taken into consideration and there is traceability in the supply chain and payments through cooperatives, and to incorporate value addition into the supply chain (Robinson and Defrenne, 2011). The traceability is an important element, allowing the EIG to ensure that the appropriate amount of money is getting to the producers (the women in the cooperatives) and that it is not being taken by middlemen or others in the supply chain. During interviews, traceability and bookkeeping was also emphasised for determining where argan fruit was collected, such that it qualifies for organic certification, as well as geographical indications protection designating that the oil is from the Souss Valley (I return to this latter point later in the chapter).

While there are several notable elements in the partnership that benefit the Amazigh women through the Targanine cooperatives (discussed further in Robinson and Defrenne, 2011; Robinson, 2014), the most relevant aspect to this ABS example is regarding the use of argan 'pressed cake'. The pressed cake is essentially a by-product of the argan oil extraction process, from which useful protein fractions have now been identified, as described in US Patent Number 7,871,766. The cooperatives sell pressed cake to BASF for approximately 15 times the local market prices. Indeed, interviews at the Targanine cooperatives revealed that the by-product is of little use to locals, except perhaps as feed for goats, or in other cooperatives it was used as a 'scrub' in soaps. This substantial 'premium' price paid for the by-product might be thought of as a fair-trade approach to ABS, or as a way of linking ABS with 'biotrade' (see Oliva, 2013). This means approximately tens of thousands of Euros were being paid annually to the cooperatives for tonnes of the pressed cake by-product, even though it has a much lower local market value at the time of interviews (2010–14).[2] The resulting payment is split such that:

- approximately 50 percent goes to a social fund for each cooperative;
- approximately 25 percent goes to the EIG of Targanine (the formal business and marketing operation of the Targanine cooperatives) for maintenance costs, machinery, investment, marketing and management; and
- approximately 25 percent goes to the cooperative (indirectly for incomes) to be spent or divided as decided by general meetings of the shareholders of the individual women's cooperatives.

The social fund of each cooperative that receives 50 percent of this premium payment for pressed cake is quite similar to other benefit-sharing funds from ABS agreements (as reviewed in Robinson, 2014). Each cooperative decides how to spend the money within the fund and so it has been allocated to a number of different purposes. For example, of the 25 percent going to the EIG, in 2011 (from the 2010 payment) the money was allocated towards logistical costs (transport from the cooperatives to the EIG), local quality control costs, packaging, paperwork costs for exportation and a profit margin for EIG. The purchase of a van to take guests (such as the Yamana in-country facilitator and myself), auditors and potential buyers to the cooperatives in 2010 was paid for from the 5 percent fair-trade premium paid for the oil at the end of the previous year. This decision was again made by consensus at an annual general meeting of the Targanine EIG (Targanine interviews, 2010, 2011, 2014).

Further to this arrangement to supply L'Oréal, argan leaves are used to derive an extract at BASF, which has a cosmetic application. The leaves are collected on parcels of argan forest on private land under a covenant with the Moroccan Water and Forests Authorities (interviews, 2010, 2011). An experimental unit was initially established in the village of Amelne, Tiznit province, south of Agadir to monitor the effects of leaf collection and the pros and cons of different leaf collection methods (Stussi et al., 2005). The covenant specifically implied commitments for maintenance of trees and reforestation of the parcel if any damage occurred. Coppicing tree maintenance operations were preferred for the collection of leaves, where they are by-products of the pruning of branches for the general maintenance of argan trees (e.g. removal of dead or dying branches). In a meeting with staff from the High Commissariat (held at the Regional Office for the South West in 2011), they indicated that they had been reluctant to allow or license groups to cut leaves from the trees, unless under strict conditions. They indicated that it might cause an enforcement problem if not carefully managed, and that they had to prevent damage to trees in the UNESCO Biosphere Reserve. The rules have had to be applied more strictly in recent years due to the booming market for argan oil, meaning that people can be fined for collecting from trees or damaging them. At the same time, most interview respondents noted that awareness of these rules was much more widespread than ten years ago, when it was common to see people damaging or cutting the trees (interviews, 2011, 2014). As a result of these concerns, in 2014, BASF had shifted to purchasing leaves from private landholders further north of the Souss region, where there are no specific protections on the forest (interview, 2014).

Benefit-sharing impacts

The Targanine social fund has been spent on a range of different expenses, as decided by each of the six cooperatives (elaborated on further in Chapters 5 and 6) (see Figures 3.3 and 3.4). These include the following:

- literacy programs (Arabic);
- health insurance fund which is only eligible for under 65-year-olds (notably, some cooperatives had not opted for health insurance to ensure equity amongst all ages of women in their cooperative);
- medical expenses for the women and families (and the cost of some surgeries);
- school supplies for children (books, pens, furniture);
- distribution of food amongst the local community;
- weddings and supplies for weddings;
- optometry testing and the purchase of eye-glasses;
- cushions and air conditioning for cooperative rooms to improve comfortability;
- pharmacy products;
- washing machines (shared at the cooperative);
- sewing machines and classes;
- playground, toys and games for children;
- blankets for families for the wintertime;
- televisions and whitegoods.

At all of the cooperatives, I asked what an average daily income would be for one of the women. This always led to detailed discussions about the

Figure 3.3 A crèche at Toudarte, one of the Targanine cooperatives

Source: Taken by the author, Daniel Robinson, 2 May 2011.

Figure 3.4 Sewing machines used for teaching and sewing clothes and blankets, Toudarte

Source: Taken by the author, Daniel Robinson, 2 May 2011.

amount paid and the number of hours worked, the time it took different women to crush the nuts, and also how much fruit each woman and her family had collected. Women who are part of Targanine are typically paid per kilogram of kernel produced (by cracking nuts), and they are also paid per kilogram of fruit collected and supplied to the cooperatives. At cooperative Toudarte, they had clearly worked out an average daily figure of 75–85 Dirham (US$10) per day for a woman producing 700 grams to 1 kilogram of kernels (a typical amount for a day's work, or approximately 7–8 hours) (figures based on interviews held in 2011, and correspondence with BASF in 2014). This figure might be even higher if the woman supplies fruit – paid at approximately 1 Dirham per kilogram. Similar figures were estimated at the other six cooperatives, or slightly lower daily rates (45 Dirham per day for a woman who was a slow worker, and 65–85 Dirham per day for women who were more efficient). 85 Dirham per day is significantly above the agricultural minimum wage of 63 Dirham (approximately US$7) per day (for up to 10 hours' work), and the women have more flexible and typically shorter working hours. This is without the additional income supplement provided by the social fund, from which the women can vote to receive a portion of this money for specific purposes (e.g. purchase of white goods), or the redistribution of yearly benefits (from the fair-trade allocation). Further to this, the members of the partnership such as EIG Targanine and Yamana have assisted with applications to the European Union for grants for the purchase of equipment for pressing the kernels, quality control and also for de-pulping the fruit (also co-financed by cooperative funds, including the social fund). This equipment results in a higher value product for sale to BASF or to other buyers (they have a non-exclusive agreement). It also means that the women are able to save time – for example, it might take a woman an entire day to manually de-pulp the outside fruit layer from one 60-kilogram sack of argan fruit (discussed further in Chapter 4). There is no income derived from de-pulping – it merely prepares the nuts for cracking. However, the purchase of de-pulping machines reduces this time to remove the dried fruit husk to about 5 to 10 minutes. By purchasing the machines (a few of the cooperatives had them as at August 2011), the women can effectively double their kernel production time and income (Robinson, 2014).

Further to this, the success of the cooperatives has meant other monetary benefits for them. To become a member of the cooperative required the women to make an upfront payment of about 400 Dirham in 2004 at Toudarte.[3] This 'share' in the cooperative is worth about 15,000 Dirham (US$1,800) in 2011, and this is continuing to climb, so when women retire from this work they can draw back their share to help them in older age.

There are clearly considerable benefits and impacts for the women in the Targanine cooperatives from the purchase of argan oil by BASF and other

European companies (biotrade) and also from the social fund for the purchase of pressed cake (from which a type of benefit-sharing occurs through a premium price paid). These are comparable to guiding provisions established under international law. For example, if we examine the Annex of the Nagoya Protocol, the list of possible monetary benefits includes: access fees/fees per sample; up-front payments and special fees to be paid into trust funds supporting conservation and sustainable use of biodiversity; and salaries and preferential terms where mutually agreed, amongst other things. Often, benefit sharing involves access or up-front fees, then milestone payments and/or royalties at the achievement of specified developmental milestones. While this case is different, the premium payment for commodity supply of argan pressed cake into a trust fund is quite similar to the suggested 'special fees' item in the Annex. In any case, the Annex to the Nagoya Protocol is a non-exclusive list and premium price for biotrade supply could well be an addition. A number of non-monetary benefits such as contributions to the local economy, social recognition, and food and livelihood security benefits are also relevant to the cooperatives. Other items from the Annex, such as joint intellectual property rights and collaboration in research, participation in product development and also technology transfer, are also relevant given the collaborations between Professor Charrouf and BASF, as well as the technology transfers made to the cooperatives (Robinson, 2014).

The benefits are felt by the women who have a share in the cooperative (e.g. at Tagmate there are approximately 40 women), with flow on benefits for their community if the women choose to spend their money in certain ways (e.g. setting up medical treatment days or eye-sight testing for the community). However, the argan trade has been so lucrative, particularly for the Targanine cooperatives that benefit from the social fund, so that now many other women wish to join, but are not able. Given that there is such demand for argan oil by local and international markets, including the bulk purchases by BASF, the cooperatives are having trouble keeping up with demand. At the time of the interviews held in 2011, the cooperatives sometimes had to purchase fruit from families and brokers in surrounding areas because the women in the cooperatives could not supply enough on their own. In addition, the cooperatives have attracted affiliated centres whereby the Targanine cooperatives had to purchase nuts from these women at standard market rates (depending upon the decisions made by that cooperative) in 2011. This has since been improved, with supply agreements being implemented between cooperatives and affiliated centres. These agreements include commitments on the price paid, an annual premium for the affiliated centre (fair trade) and access to the social fund actions.

This means that the dissemination of fair-trade payments and social fund benefits was limited to a relatively small group (approximately 240 women in all six cooperatives as at August 2011, which grew to 384 in 2012, and 557 in 2014), and this might raise questions about 'fairness and equity' of the argan oil trade overall. This rings true of the industry more broadly, with the findings of Lybbert, Barrett and Narjisse (2002, p. 125), who note that most locals 'only participate superficially in the new and expanded markets for argan oil, and the benefits that do trickle down to local households appear to be regressively distributed, both regionally and between households'.

While the cooperatives have continually expanded, the EIG explained that they can only do so at a relatively slow rate because of the risks associated with market volatility, demand and also the quantity they can obtain from the argan forest. In the ABS context, this means that the local 'providers' of the 'genetic resource' (to adopt the language of the Nagoya Protocol) are benefiting in the absence of a broader ABS framework in Morocco for, say, an ABS fund. In other circumstances, ABS funds have been established with the intent to disseminate benefits to a wide range of beneficiaries – in this case, the traditional knowledge about the cosmetic benefits of argan is widely held and so there might be a claim for wider benefit-sharing. However, the patented pressed cake extract is arguably *not* directly based on traditional knowledge because it is from a processed extract not previously used by the women. This case also differs from others because the provision of genetic resources occurs as a biotrade transaction – tonnes of pressed cake purchased by BASF and used by L'Oréal.

The original access to genetic resources for utilisation (R&D) was arguably made by Professor Charrouf, the Moroccan scientist, who then began to work with BASF and L'Oréal towards unique biochemical extracts as active ingredients for cosmetics. As a co-inventor, Professor Charrouf has received some benefit – although she indicated that the direct monetary benefits she has received have been limited. Effectively, by helping establish the EIG Targanine group, Professor Charrouf has ceded most benefits to those Amazigh women shareholders of the cooperatives. The women continue to benefit (rather than through a one-off payment, as is common for 'milestones' in commercial development of medicines in ABS agreements) because of the biotrade supply chain of both the oil and pressed cake (and, to a lesser extent, the argan leaves, where the EIG Targanine is an intermediary in the supply chain). In this sense, the agreement and supply chain are, combined, probably more successful at delivering benefits over a longer time period and to a significant number of beneficiaries than many other ABS-type agreements, precisely because they are premised on continued premium price paid for a biotrade supply of product. So, despite questions of distributional equity, it could be argued that the arrangement provides significant and life-changing benefits to a considerable number of women and their families (see Chapters 4 and 5). If this was instead put into a centralised fund to be distributed more broadly in Morocco or even the Souss Valley region, the funds might be so diluted as to be less effective (Robinson, 2014).

During the fieldwork in 2010 and 2011, I was able to interview some women in the other argan oil producing centres, to help understand the adjacent social effects of the cooperatives. Several of these women expressed that they were happy just to have work. One of the managers of a centre indicated that all of the women in her centre would like to formally be part of the EIG Targanine to receive the benefits – however, she also expressed her happiness to have the paid work. At other non-Targanine fair-trade argan-oil-producing cooperatives in the Souss Valley near Agadir, which were interviewed at a later date (in 2012 and 2014), some of the managers knew of Targanine, but did not know of the explicit benefits received or differences between their cooperatives, so there did not appear to be inter-cooperative jealousy. We explore some of these aspects further in Chapters 4 and 5.

The Nagoya Protocol to the Convention on Biological Diversity

Since conducting this fieldwork in 2010 to 2014, there have been additional developments of relevance to the ABS provisions of the Convention on Biological Diversity. These were eventually enhanced after decades of workshopping and negotiations. In 2010, the Nagoya Protocol was adopted by the Conference of the Parties to the Convention on Biological Diversity. The Nagoya Protocol then came into force in 2014 following sufficient ratifications. Morocco signed the Nagoya Protocol on 9 December 2011, but has not yet ratified it at the time of writing (in 2019).

From a legal geography perspective, I am interested in the ways in which space, place and nature are mutually co-constituted with laws. In this case, a 'legal assemblage' or a chronotope of law and nature (Valverde, 2015) can be analysed across a specific parcel of time – since the 1990s in particular, when these laws come into effect. The shift in intellectual property laws through the WTO TRIPS Agreement is a considerable change in the way private property claims can be made over components of nature. The Convention on Biological Diversity also came into place in the early 1990s and has language that rests across an awkward space between recognition of traditional knowledge of Indigenous peoples and local communities (e.g. under article 8(j)), while also recognising that intellectual property rights might be claimed over nature as 'genetic resources'. The use of genetic resources arguably commodifies plants and animals as a resource or object for exchange particularly in the 'knowledge economy' context of making intellectual property rights claims over 'value added' parts of nature (see McAfee, 1999; Whatmore, 2002; McAfee, 2003; Parry, 2004). It specifically allows for claim-making and it might be thought of as sometimes underpinned by what Drahos (1996, p. 200) describes as a 'proprietarian creed' – where property thinking and the compartmentalisation of everything into forms of private property dominates the policy landscape.

The Convention on Biological Diversity also recognises 'sovereign rights over biological resources', which is an extension of United Nations Declarations made following World War II over 'Permanent Sovereignty over Natural Resources'. However, this is highly problematic for many of the world's Indigenous peoples, who have had their customary laws, rights, relationships and responsibilities to nature colonised, and remain in often adversarial or tense Indigenous–state relations (as is sometimes the case for Amazigh–state relations). Consequently, both the Convention on Biological Diversity – and then the Nagoya Protocol after it – walk a middle road between acknowledging the capitalist knowledge economy through 'utilization of genetic resources' and related intellectual property claims, while also encouraging states to recognise and assert the rights of Indigenous peoples and local communities to ensure permissions and benefit sharing for access to genetic resources and traditional knowledge (see e.g. Nagoya Protocol, articles 5.2, 6.2, 7 and 12). This complex legal assemblage is arguably a combined result of life sciences industrial advancement (Dutfield, 2002), legal responses to proprietarian lobbying by those industries (Drahos, 2002; Sell, 2002), those who sought to find a 'win-win' for the funding of conservation through bioprospecting activities (Reid et al., 1993), and then also those who lobbied to have Indigenous rights recognised relating to nature and knowledge (Bavikatte and Robinson, 2011). The ready exchangeability of both the 'resources' and the knowledge on the one hand facilitates open trade and use. On the other hand, the constraints placed on specific uses of resources and knowledge by the intellectual property system, particularly patents, inhibit this exchange in defence of private property rights for innovation. The perceived inequity of this situation has then led to a re-regulation of the biological resources in the Nagoya Protocol, with its mandate for 'fair and equitable benefit-sharing', which might be thought of as a regulation made in favour of a 'moral economy' approach (see e.g. Scott, 1977; Goodman, 2004). Within the text of the Nagoya Protocol is a classic legal geography example of the complex mutual co-constitution of law and nature, as influenced by science and commercial interests, as well as Indigenous peoples, and conservationists and others. While there are likely to be those who are critical of this regulatory construction and some of the neoliberal influences behind it (e.g. Lybbert, 2007; Turner, 2014), it is important to note that Indigenous peoples did influence the outcome in the Nagoya Protocol (Bavikatte and Robinson, 2011), and that it does provide a mechanism for traditional knowledge protections – albeit constrained in scope (see also Robinson, 2014). One very significant component of the Nagoya Protocol in this regard is article 12, which encourages the recognition of customary laws. In the context of the argan forest and argan oil production, it would be important in Morocco for Amazigh customary laws to be recognised in a parallel manner to the provisions within the Moroccan Forestry Code, as relating to the UNESCO Biosphere Reserve listing.

An important aspect of thinking about legal assemblages is in understanding their material effects and impacts through the 'nomosphere' (Delaney, 2010) – the social/spatial mechanisms that respond to and from legal meanings and norms, and their results. These broader international legal developments have shaped the response in Morocco by the companies involved, and also to some extent by the government. The Nagoya Protocol has international compliance mechanisms that mean that countries that have ratified it are required to ensure that companies operating in their jurisdiction are respecting the ABS laws of other countries, thus providing for reciprocity in compliance (articles 15 and 16). The European Union has ratified the Nagoya Protocol and has ABS regulations in place[4] – and these have the effect of pushing compliance down supply chains – for example, from larger cosmetics companies to intermediaries, to local suppliers (see Robinson and von Braun, 2019). Given the proximity of Morocco to Europe, there is considerable trade between the two jurisdictions, and so it is likely that Morocco could benefit from the reciprocal protection mechanism under the Nagoya Protocol. But, to date, Morocco is still a signatory and has not yet ratified the Nagoya Protocol, with some projects domestically underway to assist with this process.

For example, Morocco has undertaken some regulatory analysis, consultation and capacity-building workshops in order to scope and develop an ABS regulatory framework (which typically involves drafting policies, permit systems and legislation). This has been further funded and encouraged by a number of development assistance projects from the German Development Implementation Agency (GIZ),[5] the European Union and GIZ-led multi-donor ABS Capacity Development Initiative,[6] and a United Nations Environment Program (UNEP) project as funded by the Global Environment Facility (GEF-4) on the valorisation of genetic resources and the Nagoya Protocol.[7] Morocco has a Draft Law on ABS (*Avant Projet de loi no. 56-17 sur l'accès aux ressources génétiques et le partage juste et équitable des avantages découlant de leur utilisation*), which was developed in 2017 and which has passed through parliament with approval, and it has a

National Focal Point.[8] At the time of writing (2019), the country is reputedly on the verge of ratification of the Nagoya Protocol, and finalisation of their ABS law.

The WIPO IGC and WTO forums

There have also been international forums which discuss these issues, such as the World Intellectual Property Organization (WIPO) Intergovernmental Committee on Intellectual property and Genetic Resources, Traditional Knowledge and Folklore (IGC). This is another legal norm-setting forum within the United Nations context, which governs the architecture for intellectual property filings globally. While this forum has been an important place for negotiation of policy on traditional knowledge and for raising concerns of Indigenous peoples, local communities and biodiverse developing countries, it has been progressing rather slowly since the year 2000 to have achieved only drafts of potential legal instruments for protection of Indigenous knowledge (see Robinson et al., 2017; Wendland, 2017). One major issue in this forum is that the voices of the Indigenous populations that attend are subjugated to 'observer status' and may only speak last during IGC sessions, and they may not vote on motions. The forum is therefore dominated by state-centric discussions and more generally framed within the predominant Euro-American intellectual property frameworks. This means that there are limited opportunities for the plural legal regimes that exist in many societies to permeate the dominant intellectual property and 'trade-related' norms in the forums. However, a number of Indigenous peoples as well as experts have raised customary law as a key mechanism for the protection of traditional knowledge, and the WIPO Secretariat includes a number of these documents as supporting the work of the IGC.[9] These documents highlight that customary laws are often described as 'living laws' (Tobin, 2014) because they have developed through dynamic interactions among people, place and nature. This means they are typically ideal for the protection of Indigenous and traditional knowledge of local communities, as well as being important for Indigenous self-determination (see Robinson and Graham, 2018).

While some reforms – such as patent disclosure of origin requirements – have been suggested in the IGC forum and also by many countries on the WTO TRIPS Council, the forums have been unable to reach consensus.[10] The disclosure of origin patent requirement has been argued by many experts and negotiators, particularly those from the Global South (see Bagley, 2017), as a way of ensuring that researchers and companies that file patents which utilise genetic resources and associated traditional knowledge have obtained appropriate permissions (that is, prior informed consent – PIC) and that they have an ABS agreement with the appropriate providers. This procedure has been argued for by many experts to support transparency in the patent system and reduce the risk of biopiracy, and as a result the majority of countries in the WIPO IGC and WTO TRIPS Council have indicated support for it.[11] In addition, more than 30 countries have independently established their own disclosure requirement as a 'check and balance' that supports the intent and implementation of the Nagoya Protocol.[12]

Prior to the Nagoya Protocol's entry into force, Lybbert (2007) provided a useful 'counterfactual' about patent disclosure requirements and benefit-sharing. Some of the points from the article are now moot because of the adoption of the Nagoya Protocol, with its substantial compliance mechanisms and clearing house. However, the article does raise several currently relevant and accurate points. First, the article urges caution about so-called 'blockbuster' windfalls from patents, including those relating to argan-related products. As noted above, and in the following chapters, there are substantial benefits for argan-producing cooperatives, but these are not in the order of millions of dollars (and thus arguably not 'blockbuster' status). The ABS model for the cosmetics industry is very different from what it might be in the pharmaceutical industry. In pharmaceuticals, there are very long timelines for R&D, but once a patentable drug reaches the market, if it is a 'blockbuster' drug, it can be worth tens of millions or even billions of dollars (see Ten Kate and Laird, 2019). In reality, royalty rates are often low, and can be single digits in ABS agreements (see Robinson, 2014, for several examples), so even for 'blockbuster' drugs the return is not always as expected. Therefore, restraint needs to be cautioned, given the (un)likely extent of huge benefits in the ABS context. Lybbert (2007) also highlights that there can be considerable costs in establishing an ABS regime (and also patent disclosure requirements – PDRs) and that the PDRs should be assessed based on the additional compliance incentives they may provide. It is worth noting, though, that most proponents of disclosure requirements in the WIPO IGC have argued that it would be much more efficient to have a global requirement in WIPO patent treaties or through an amendment to the TRIPS Agreement, rather than bits and pieces of patent disclosure regulation that will not necessarily provide any sort of global compliance benefit (see Oldham et al., 2013; Bagley, 2017; Chiarolla, 2019). Last, Lybbert (2007, p. 12) suggests that 'the alternative to no PDRs and no regime is not zero benefits' and in the argan case we can see that this is true; many of the benefits in relation to the argan trade that we are discussing here relate to the production of argan oil, fair-trade benefits, and the flow-on benefits from argan production and cooperatives generally, in the absence of an ABS regime in Morocco. Rather, the additional benefits from the L'Oréal/BASF arrangements with Targanine are an important recognition of the contributions of Amazigh women to both the argan forest and argan innovation, and provide moderate benefits to those cooperatives. However, as noted above, the European Union's ABS regulations *are* likely to force 'users' of genetic resource and traditional knowledge-based products to share benefits down supply chains (Robinson and von Braun, 2019). This could therefore see more ABS agreements come into effect in the coming years under the Nagoya Protocol regime. This is particularly the case if the Moroccan government has even basic ABS policy and regulations in place, because researchers who do not comply with the Moroccan rules could then be penalised at home under the European Union's compliance mechanism. Any PDR that might be developed would then be a mechanism through which to monitor and catch those who are non-compliant (i.e. those who are patenting new natural products, but who have not sought PIC or received a permit and established a benefit-sharing agreement with Moroccan agencies or provider groups).

Indications of geographical origin and naming conflicts

Related to some of these concerns is the current production of argan oil products in countries other than Morocco, where the argan tree is endemic. In 1985, Israeli researchers started planting argan crops in the Negev Desert of Israel (Nerd et al., 1994; Nerd et al., 1998) and there has been ongoing monitoring of these orchards for plant growth and fruit production ever since. After three to four years, there was some fruit yield and, in the mid-to-late 1990s, the researchers started selection of high-yielding clones with suitable agricultural traits such as a single trunk, regular flowering period and good fruit yield with high oil content, for propagation (Nerd et al., 1994; Nerd et al., 1998). The researchers noted challenges with a Fusariam disease in dry, wilting branches, which is typically caused by a fungal pathogen found in soil around the world (*Fusarium oxysporum*) (Nerd et al., 1994) and, in interviews with cooperatives, some of the managers speculated that these were persistent issues for the Israeli argan farmers or that there were mycorrhizal and root problems in Israel (interviews, 2014). Other interviewees suggested there were some small-scale argan orchards or experimental plots in Mexico, although there is only limited evidence about this (Orwa et al., 2015).

From Israel, the trademarked brand 'Moroccan Oil' is one of the most distinctive and dominant brands containing argan oil. The founder of 'Moroccan Oil' – Chilean-born entrepreneur Carmen Tal – has indicated they came upon argan oil 'not through years of research', but 'by accident' in a Tel Aviv hair salon (CNN, 2012; Soetan, 2012). As Soetan (2012) explains: 'Her strategy was simple: take the best of Africa to the rest of the world. She and her now ex-husband, Ofer, bought the small Israeli company that imported argan oil from Morocco just a year after her first treatment and began importing to North America.' As the demand for the product has grown, the CEO explains that their company also produces 80 percent of their product in Israel, which involves a 'secret formula' – including argan oil (CNN, 2012). This raises the question of whether Israeli production has now replaced Moroccan imports to Israel, and whether Morocco still stands to benefit from a product that uses the country's name to sell itself.

Interestingly, in interviews with many of the cooperatives in 2014, some of the respondents did not seem concerned by the production in Israel:

> We have lots of festivals here for the Jewish people. There is a strong connection between the two countries. The counsel of the King is Jewish. We kept the Jews safe during the war, and saved them. There may be competition, yes, but it is not a problem . . . Israeli argan will not be like Moroccan Argan. It is the soil and region that makes it unique.
>
> (Targanine cooperative director, September 2014)

> In Israel they don't have cooperatives, they have a factory. It is not the same. We could teach them how to crack the nuts. I started when I was a young girl with my mother. We made it at home traditionally, and even sold it at the local market. We could sell it with other fruits and vegetables back then. There is a generation to generation transfer with argan.
>
> (cooperative member, Targanine cooperative, September 2014)

On the one side of the responses, there is a distinct connection between Moroccan, and particularly Amazigh people, and the Jewish people, which was being used to diffuse concern about the potential appropriation of argan trees from Morocco to Israel. In Morocco, there are holidays and ceremonies such as Uday-n Tashurt (or Jewish *Ashura*), where Amazigh people have ritually performed Jewish characters and demonstrated philo-Semitic nostalgia for a former Jewish presence (Silverstein, 2011). Amazigh activists' ideological self-positioning as anti-Islamist moderns also aligns well with Jewish ideas. They see in the Zionist movement a model for the Amazigh struggle: the successful codification and preservation of a threatened language, the obtaining of political and territorial autonomy with the establishment of the State of Israel (Silverstein, 2011; 2012).

The other side of the responses is more focused on the uniqueness of the *terroir* of the Souss Valley of Morocco and the cultural heritage transferred from generation to generation for the production of argan. This latter response aligns well with ideas within the Moroccan argan sector for protection of a geographical indication of origin filing for *Argane* (discussed below).

Trademarks for 'Moroccan Oil' or similar products have been filed and granted in several countries (e.g. US Patent and Trademark Office Serial number 77122509, registration number 3478807, filed on 5 March 2007, registered 5 August 2008).[13] The WIPO Global Brand Database notes dozens of active, inactive and pending trademarks for the brand, registered or filed for assessment in many countries for several of the company's products.[14] The Madrid System (established under the Madrid Agreement Concerning the International Registration of Marks, 1891, and Madrid Protocol, 1989, as administered by WIPO) allows for registering and managing trademarks worldwide, with a single application and set of fees to apply for protection in up to 121 countries (WIPO, 2019).

This situation raises additional legal and ethical questions surrounding the trademarks, about whether they are deceptive about the origins of production and thus fundamentally unfair given the origins of the Indigenous knowledge (also given the global emphasis on ABS frameworks). If granted, these trademarks can be highly restrictive on other businesses that might want to use the same or a similar brand name or design/logo. Although they require renewal, trademarks can in theory continue to provide protection in perpetuity if they continue to be used and the relevant fees paid. But not all countries have granted the trademarks to this company. In a recent case in Australia (*Aldi Foods Pty Ltd v. Moroccanoil Israel Ltd* [2018] FCAFC 93), the Full Federal Court found the trademark application to be 'descriptive' or, in other words, a generic description of a particular good that is not particularly adapted to distinguish the product from others. The Federal Court also found that the word 'MOROCCANOIL' was not to any extent inherently adapted to distinguish Moroccanoil's hair-care products from the goods of other traders. This was because:

- the words 'Moroccan', 'Morocco' and 'oil' were all being used extensively by other traders in connection with argan-oil hair-care products prior to the date of application for the trademark;
- there were legitimate reasons for a trader to market an argan-oil hair-care product as Moroccan Oil or by reference to the fact that it was an oil sourced from Morocco; and
- as at the date of application, argan oil was at least associated with, if not actually derived from, Morocco and thus was descriptive of an ingredient in hair-care products (Gerakiteys and Chan, 2019).

These types of issue have led to an attempt by Moroccan producers and the Moroccan government to protect a geographical indication (GI) of argan oil

(Réviron and El Benni, 2012; WIPO 2015). The unique geographical and environmental conditions in which the argan tree grows, coupled with the Amazigh traditional knowledge associated with its use, and the importance of the tree to Amazigh and Arab Moroccans has led to this GI registration. WIPO (2019) explains that a GI:

> . . . is a sign used on products that have a specific geographical origin and possess qualities or a reputation that are due to that origin. In order to function as a GI, a sign must identify a product as originating in a given place. In addition, the qualities, characteristics or reputation of the product should be essentially due to the place of origin. Since the qualities depend on the geographical place of production, there is a clear link between the product and its original place of production.

This is underpinned by the French concept of *terroir* and based on earlier concepts of appellations of origin in Europe.

The Association Marocaine de l'Industrie Géographique de l'Huile d'Argane (AMIGHA) was established to register and enforce a GI, leading to an application to the European Union to protect *argane* (argan in French) with the support of the Moroccan government (see Saber, 2008; 2010). The application for *argane* to become a Protected Geographical Indication (PGI) was made in October 2011 with the European Commission; however, the application for GI still does not seem to be approved.[15] If approved, *argane* could be one of the first PGIs from Africa to receive such protection within the European Union's regulatory framework. A PGI registration would identify *argane* as being from a specific region, with resulting unique properties, and would signal to consumers that its production meets specific standards.

Despite positive reporting (see WIPO, 2015), I have heard mixed stories about progress on GI protection of argan during fieldwork (2014) and afterwards. It seems that while reciprocal GI protection has been registered between Morocco and the European Union, the association in Morocco has been disestablished or has collapsed, and interview responses indicated the GI protection was only having limited effect. Attempts to contact AMIGHA have repeatedly failed (2015–19). In my interviews with several argan cooperatives and businesses, I questioned them about these external laws, 'Moroccan Oil' and the Israeli argan orchards and potential foreign production activity. While some people in argan businesses and cooperatives had not heard about these foreign activities, most had. In several responses, the cooperative managers and women said they were not concerned about the foreign production, which I will return to in Chapter 6.

Summary

The unique biological, ecological and cultural significance of the argan tree, due to its traditional uses in the Souss Valley, have significantly influenced the arrangement of legal regimes within Morocco, and thus provide a clear example of the co-constitution of law and geography. These legal arrangements have in turn become part of broader legal assemblages that draw upon supra-state influences from the UNESCO frameworks, global intellectual property laws and from the Nagoya Protocol and the Convention on Biological Diversity. Significantly, these have also been shifted in specific ways by the advancement of scientific research on natural products, including the use of argan in cosmetics, and by the commercial interests behind much of this research. While there have been attempts within Morocco (e.g. GIs) and through benefit-sharing in supply chains to improve local benefits and to protect and promote the local producers, there still remains a lopsidedness in power relations and limitations in the legal regimes for the establishment of a more broad-scale 'moral economy' (Goodman, 2004) for the local argan producers. At least for the ABS regime, it is still a work in progress at the time of writing. The identification of argan 'not by years of research, but by accident' (CNN, 2012), which led to the development of Moroccan Oil products – and then attempts to register widely what is arguably a generic and deceptive trademark – is particularly indicative of the ongoing global structural inequities operating in advanced capitalism, using the tools of dominant intellectual property regimes to pursue individualistic and opportunistic proprietarianism. This sort of commercial activity has been described by some as 'accumulation by dispossession' (Harvey, 2003, p. 137; see also Turner, 2014). While attempts to protect and promote traditional knowledge and the production of the Moroccan argan cooperatives (such as through the ABS arrangement and the geographical indications protection) have a role to play, arguably these frameworks may not be sufficient in scale or scope to fully recognise the contributions of the Amazigh people and the local *terroir*.

Notes

1 Forestry management in Morocco is governed by the forestry code, which derives from the *Dahir relatif à la protection et à l'exploitation des forets* (Law of Forest Protection and Exploitation) issued under French protectorate in 1917 (Aubert et al., 2009).
2 Exact figures were provided by the Targanine cooperatives, but members of the tripartite partnership requested that this information not be publicly disclosed for commercial-in-confidence reasons.
3 It should be noted that Toudarte is probably the most successful of the six cooperatives, and so the shares may not be worth as much at the other cooperatives.

4 For more information, see Regulation (EU) No. 511/2014 of the European Parliament and of the Council on compliance measures for users from the Nagoya Protocol on Access to Genetic Resources and the Fair and Equitable Sharing of Benefits Arising from their Utilization in the Union was adopted on 16 April 2014, and entered into force 12 October 2014.

5 For more information about GIZ projects, see <http://www.secheresse.info/spip.php?article76717>.

6 For more information, see <http://www.abs-initiative.info/countries-and-regions/africa/morocco/>.

7 For more information on the UNEP GEF-4 project, see <https://www.cbd.int/countries/profile/default.shtml?country=ma>.

8 For more information, see the national focal point website: <http://ma.chm-cbd.net/protocole-nagoya>. At the time of writing (2019), much of this website was a work in progress. The Nagoya Protocol Clearing House portal page for Morocco can be found at <https://absch.cbd.int/countries/MA/MSR>.

9 For more information, see the following WIPO resources: <https://www.wipo.int/tk/en/indigenous/customary_law/index.html>; <https://www.wipo.int/edocs/pubdocs/en/wipo_pub_tk_7.pdf>; and <https://www.wipo.int/export/sites/www/tk/en/resources/pdf/overview_customary_law.pdf>.

10 For more information, see the WTO fact sheets and submissions available at <https://www.wto.org/english/tratop_e/trips_e/art27_3b_background_e.htm>.

11 For more information, see recent submissions and reports of the WIPO IGC, which is now past its 40th session: <https://www.wipo.int/tk/en/news/igc/2019/news_0009.html>.

12 For more information, WIPO has compiled a May 2019 table of disclosure of origin requirements: <https://www.wipo.int/export/sites/www/tk/en/documents/pdf/genetic_resources_disclosure.pdf>.

13 For more information, see US Trademark Electronic Search System (TESS) search for 'Moroccanoil': <http://tmsearch.uspto.gov>.

14 For more information, see WIPO Global Brand Database search for 'Moroccanoil': <https://www3.wipo.int/branddb/en/>.

15 For more information, see the EU Agriculture and Rural Development portal, 'Argane' application: <https://ec.europa.eu/agriculture/quality/door/appliedName.html?denominationId=4900>.

References

African Group IP/C/W/404. 'Taking Forward the Review of Article 27.3(b) of the TRIPS Agreement' submitted 26 June 2003; and also Communication from Bolivia IP/C/W/545 Review of Article 27.3(b) of the TRIPS Agreement 26 February 2010, <https://www.wto.org/english/tratop_e/trips_e/art27_3b_e.htm>.

ANDZOA/INRA (2015, 17–19 December). *Résumés du Communications 3ème Congrès International de l'Arganier*, Agadir: ANDZOA/INRA, <http://www.congresarganier.ma/pdf/Cia2015/Recueil_des_communications.pdf>.

Aubert, P. M., Leroy, M. and Auclair, L. (2009). Moroccan Forestry Policies and Local Forestry Management in the High Atlas: A Cross Analysis of Forestry Administration and Local Institutions. *Small-scale Forestry*, 8(2), 175–191.

Bagley, M. A. (2017). Of Disclosure 'Straws' and IP System 'Camels'. In D.F. Robinson, P. Roffe and A. Abdel-Latif (eds). *Protecting Traditional Knowledge: The WIPO Intergovernmental Committee on Intellectual Property and Genetic Resources, Traditional Knowledge and Folklore* (pp. 85–107). Abingdon, Oxon: Routledge.

Bartel, R., Graham, N., Jackson, S., Prior, J., Robinson, D., Sherval, M. and Williams, S. (2013). Legal Geography: An Australian Perspective. *Geographical Research*, 51(4), pp. 339–353.

Bartel, R. and Graham, N. (2016). Property and Place Attachment: A Legal Geographical Analysis of Biodiversity Law Reform in New South Wales. *Geographical Research*, 54(3), pp. 267–284.

Bavikatte, K. and Robinson, D. (2011). Towards a People's History of the Law: Biocultural Jurisprudence and the Nagoya Protocol on Access and Benefit Sharing. *Law Environment and Development Journal*, 7(1), pp. 35–51.

Bennett, L. and Layard, A. (2015). Legal Geography: Becoming Spatial Detectives. *Geography Compass*, 9(7), pp. 406–422.

Blomley, N. (1994). *Law, Space, and the Geographies of Power*. New York and London: Guilford Press.

Bonn Guidelines on Access to Genetic Resources and Fair and Equitable Sharing of the Benefits Arising out of their Utilization (2002). Montreal: CBD Secretariat and UNEP, <https://www.cbd.int/doc/publications/cbd-bonn-gdls-en.pdf>.

Bellefontaine, R. (2010). De la domestication à l'amélioration variétale de L'arganier (Argania spinosa L. Skeels)? *Sécheresse*, 21(1), pp. 42–53.

Braverman, I. (2014). Introduction. In I. Braverman, N. Blomley, D. Delaney and A. Kedar (eds). *The Expanding Spaces of Law: A Timely Legal Geography* (pp. 1–22). Redwood City, California: Stanford University Press.

Braverman, I. (2017). Lively Legalities. In I. Braverman (ed.). *Animals, Biopolitics, Law: Lively Legalities* (pp. 3–18). Abingdon, Oxon: Routledge.

Charrouf, Z. and Guillaume, D. (1999). Ethnoeconomical, Ethnomedical, and Phytochemical Study of Argania spinosa (L.) Skeels. *Journal of Ethnopharmacology*, 67(1), pp. 7–14.

Charrouf, Z. and Guillaume, D. (2009). Sustainable Development in Northern Africa: The Argan Forest Case. *Sustainability*, 1(4), pp. 1012–1022.

Chiarolla, C. (2019). Intellectual Property from a Global Environmental Law Perspective: Lessons from Patent Disclosure Requirements for Genetic Resources and Traditional Knowledge. *Transnational Environmental Law*, 8(3), pp. 503–521.

CNN (2012, 30 September). Made in Israel: Moroccan Oil, <https://edition.cnn.com/videos/bestoftv/2012/06/01/exp-eb-israel-moroccan-oil.cnn 30/9/2019>.

Convention on Biological Diversity (1992). <https://www.cbd.int/>.

Davies, M. (2012). Legal Pluralism. In P. Cane and H. Kritzer (eds). *The Oxford Handbook of Empirical Legal Research* (pp. 804–825). Oxford: Oxford University Press.

Davies, M. (2017). *Law Unlimited: Materialism, Pluralism, and Legal Theory*. Abingdon, Oxon: Routledge.

Delaney, D. (2003). *Law and Nature*. Cambridge and New York: Cambridge University Press.

Delaney, D. (2010). *The Spatial, the Legal and the Pragmatics of World-Making: Nomospheric Investigations*. Abingdon, Oxon: Routledge.

Delaney, D. (2015). Legal Geography I: Constitutivities, Complexities, and Contingencies. *Progress in Human Geography*, 39(1), pp. 96–102.

Delaney, D. (2016). Legal Geography II: Discerning Injustice. *Progress in Human Geography*, 40(2), pp. 267–274.

Drahos, P. (1996). *A Philosophy of Intellectual Property*. Aldershot: Ashgate.

Drahos, P. with Braithwaite, J. (2002). *Information Feudalism: Who Owns the Knowledge Economy*. London: Earthscan.

Dutfield, G. (2002). *Intellectual Property Rights and the Life Science Industries: A 20th Century History*. Aldershot: Ashgate.

Gerakiteys, D. and Chan, C. (2019, 30 August). You Can't Register That as a Trademark! A Win from the Discount Bin for Aldi, <https://www.claytonutz.com/knowledge/2018/august/you-cant-register-that-as-a-trade-mark-a-win-from-the-discount-bin-for-aldi>.

Gillespie, J. (2016). Catch 22: Wetlands Protection and Fishing for Survival. *Geographical Research*, 54(3), pp. 336–347.

Goodman, M. (2004). Reading Fair Trade: Political Ecological Imaginary and the Moral Economy of Fair Trade Foods. *Political Geography*, 23(7), pp. 891–915.

Harry, D. (2011). Biocolonialism and Indigenous Knowledge in United Nations Discourse. *Griffith Law Review*, 20(3), pp. 702–728.

Harvey, D. (2003). *The New Imperialism*. Oxford: Oxford University Press.

Hayden, C. (2003). *When Nature Goes Public: The Making and Unmaking of Bioprospecting in Mexico*. Princeton, NJ: Princeton University Press.

High Commissariat for Water and Forests, and the Fight Against Desertification (2019). Regulations webpage, <http://www.eauxetforets.gov.ma/Legislation/Reglement/Pages/Textes-Reglementaires.aspx#>.

Institut de Recherche pour le Développement (IRD) (2011). The Moroccan Arganeraie Shaped by Human Endeavour. IRD Scientific Newssheets, no. 367, <https://en.ird.fr/the-media-centre/scientific-newssheets/367-the-moroccan-arganeraie-shaped-by-human-endeavour>.

Lybbert, T. J., Barrett, C. B. and Narjisse, H. (2002). Market-Based Conservation and Local Benefits: The Case of Argan Oil in Morocco. *Ecological Economics*, 41(1), pp. 125–144.

Lybbert, T., Barrett, C. and Narjisse, H. (2004). Does Resource Commercialization Induce Local Conservation? A Cautionary Tale from Southwestern Morocco. *Society & Natural Resources*, 17(5), pp. 413–430.

Lybbert, T. (2007). Patent Disclosure Requirements and Benefit Sharing: A Counterfactual Case of Morocco's Argan Oil. *Ecological Economics*, 64(1), pp. 12–18.

Marrakesh Agreement Establishing the World Trade Organization: Annex 1C Trade-Related Aspects of Intellectual Property Rights (1994). <https://www.wto.org/english/docs_e/legal_e/27-trips_01_e.htm>.

McAfee, K. (1999). Selling Nature to Save It? Biodiversity and Green Developmentalism. *Environment and Planning D: Society and Space*, 17(2), pp. 133–154.

McAfee, K. (2003). Neoliberalism on the Molecular Scale. Economic and Genetic Reductionism in Biotechnology Battles. *Geoforum*, 34(2), pp. 203–219.

McGown, J. (2006). *Out of Africa: Mysteries of Access and Benefit Sharing*. Washington, DC: Edmonds Institute.

Morgera, E., Tsioumani, E. and Buck, M. (2014). *Unravelling the Nagoya Protocol: A Commentary on the Nagoya Protocol on Access and Benefit-Sharing to the Convention on Biological Diversity*. Leiden, Netherlands: Brill/Martinus Nijhoff.

Nagoya Protocol on Access to Genetic Resources and the Fair and Equitable Sharing of Benefits Arising from their Utilization to the Convention on Biological Diversity (2010). <https://www.cbd.int/abs/doc/protocol/nagoya-protocol-en.pdf>.

Nerd, A., Eteshola, E., Borowy, N. and Mizrahi, Y. (1994). Growth and Oil Production of Argan in the Negev Desert of Israel. *Industrial Crops and Products*, 2(2), pp. 89–95.

Nerd, A., Irijimovich, V. and Mizrahi, Y. (1998). Phenology, Breeding System and Fruit Development of Argan [Argania spinosa, Sapotaceae] Cultivated in Israel. *Economic Botany*, 52(2), pp. 161–167.

O'Donnell, T. (2016). Legal Geography and Coastal Climate Change Adaptation: The Vaughan Litigation. *Geographical Research*, 54(3), pp. 301–312.

O'Donnell, T., Robinson, D. and Gillespie, J. (2020). Introduction: What's Different about the Australasian and Asia-Pacific Approach to Legal Geography? In T. O'Donnell, D. Robinson and J. Gillespie (eds). *Legal Geography: Perspectives and Methods* (pp. 3–16). Abingdon, Oxon: Routledge.

Oldham, P., Hall, S. and Forero, O. (2013). Biological Diversity in the Patent System. *PloS one*, 8(11), e78737.

Oliva, M. (2013). The Implications of the Nagoya Protocol for the Ethical Sourcing of Biodiversity. In E. Morgera, M. Buck and E. Tsioumani (eds). *The 2010 Nagoya Protocol on Access and Benefit-Sharing in Perspective Implications for International Law and Implementation Challenges* (pp. 371–388). Leiden: Martinus Nijhoff.

Orwa, C., Mutua, A., Kindt, R., Jamnadass, R. and Anthony, S. (2015, 28 December). *Agroforestree Database: A Tree Reference and Selection Guide Version 4.0*, <http://www.worldagroforestry.org/publication/agroforestree-database-tree-species-reference-and-selection-guide-version-40>.

Parry, B. (2004). *Trading the Genome: Investigating the Commodification of Bio-information*. New York: Columbia University Press.

Proulx, C. (2005). Blending Justice: Interlegality and the Incorporation of Aboriginal Justice into the Formal Canadian Justice System. *Journal of Legal Pluralism and Unofficial Law*, 37(51), pp. 79–109.

Reid, W., Laird, S., Meyer, C., Gámez, R., Sittenfeld, A., Janzen, D. and Juma, C. (1993). *Biodiversity Prospecting: Using Genetic Resources for Sustainable Development*, 333.716(R359). Washington DC: World Resources Institute.

Réviron, S. and El Benni, N. (2012). Morocco: Argan Oil. In M. Blakeney (ed). *Extending the Protection of Geographical Indications: Case Studies of Agricultural Products in Africa* (pp. 255–265). London: Earthscan.

Robinson, D. (2010). *Confronting Biopiracy: Cases, Challenges and International Debates*. London: Earthscan and Routledge.

Robinson, D. and Defrenne, E. (2011). *Argan: A Case Study on ABS*. Amsterdam: Union for Ethical Biotrade.

Robinson, D. F. (2013). Legal Geographies of Intellectual Property, 'Traditional' Knowledge and Biodiversity: Experiencing Conventions, Laws, Customary Law, and Karma in Thailand. *Geographical Research*, 51(4), pp. 375–386.

Robinson, D. F. (2014). *Biodiversity, Access and Benefit-Sharing: Global Case Studies*. Abingdon, Oxon: Routledge.

Robinson, D. F., Roffe, P. and Abdel-Latif, A. (2017). Introduction: Mapping the Evolution, State-of-Play and Future of the WIPO IGC. In D. F. Robinson, P. Roffe and A. Abdel-Latif (eds). *Protecting Traditional Knowledge: The WIPO Intergovernmental Committee on Intellectual Property and Genetic Resources, Traditional Knowledge and Folklore* (pp. 3–9). Abingdon, Oxon: Routledge.

Robinson, D., Abdel-Latif, A. and Roffe, P. (eds) (2017). *Protecting Traditional Knowledge: The WIPO Intergovernmental Committee on Intellectual Property and Genetic Resources, Traditional Knowledge and Folklore*. Abingdon, Oxon: Routledge.

Robinson, D. and Graham, N. (2018). Legal Pluralisms, Justice and Spatial Conflicts: New Directions in Legal Geography. *Geographical Journal*, 184(1), pp. 3–7.

Robinson, D. and von Braun, J. (2019). New Challenges for the Nagoya Protocol: Diverging Implementation Regimes for Access and Benefit-Sharing. In C. Correa and X. Sueba (eds). *Intellectual Property and Development: Understanding the Interfaces* (pp. 377–403). Singapore: Springer.

Saber, M. (2008, 14 February). Agadir: L'huile d'argan dotée d'une appellation géographique protégée, *Aujourd'hui Le Maroc*, <http://www.aujourdhui.ma/actualite-details59857.html> accessed 7 March 2011.

Saber, M. (2010, 17 May). Souss-Massa-Draa: l'indication geographique protégée 'Argane' est operationelle, *Aujourd'hui Le Maroc*, <http://www.maghress.com/fr/aujourdhui/75925>.

Santos, B. (1987). Law: A Map of Misreading. Toward a Postmodern Conception of Law. *Journal of Law and Society*, 14(3), pp. 279–302.

Santos, B. (2002). *Toward a New Legal Common Sense* (2nd edition). London: Butterworths.

Scott, J. (1977). *The Moral Economy of the Peasant: Rebellion and Subsistence in Southeast Asia*. New Haven, Connecticut: Yale University Press.

Sell, S. (2002). Industry Strategies for Intellectual Property and Trade: The Quest for TRIPS, and Post-TRIPS Strategies. *Cardozo Journal of International & Comparative Law*, 10(79), pp. 79–108.

Silverstein, P. (2011). Masquerade Politics: Race, Islam and the Scale of Amazigh Activism in Southeastern Morocco. *Nations and Nationalism*, 17(1), pp. 65–84.

Silverstein, P. A. (2012). A New Morocco? Amazigh Activism, Political Pluralism and Anti–Anti-Semitism. *Brown Journal of World Affairs*, 18(2), pp. 129–140.

Soetan, F. (2012, 16 December). *Mining Liquid Gold: Carmen Tal, CEO Moroccan Oil*, <http://venturesafrica.com/mining-liquid-gold-carmen-tal-ceo-moroccanoil/>.

Stussi, I., Henry, F., Moser, P., Danoux, L., Jeanmarie, C., Gillon, V., Benoit, I., Charrouf, Z. and Paully, G. (2005). Argania Spinosa – How Ecological Farming, Fair Trade and Sustainability Can Drive the Research for New Cosmetic Active Ingredients. *SOFW Journal*, 131(10), pp. 35–46.

Ten Kate, K. and Laird, S. (2019). *The Commercial Use of Biodiversity: Access to Genetic Resources and Benefit-Sharing*. London: Routledge.

Tobin, B. (2014). *Indigenous Peoples, Customary Law and Human Rights – Why Living Law Matters*. Abingdon, Oxon: Routledge.

Turner, B. (2014). Neoliberal Politics of Resource Extraction: Moroccan Argan Oil. *Forum for Development Studies,* 41(2), pp. 207–232.

Turner, B. (2016). Supply-Chain Legal Pluralism: Normativity as Constitutive of Chain Infrastructure in the Moroccan Argan Oil Supply Chain. *Journal of Legal Pluralism and Unofficial Law*, 48(3), pp. 378–414.

Turner, B. (2017). Translating Evidentiary Practices and Technologies of Truth Finding: Oath Taking as Witness Testimony in Plural Legal Configurations in Rural Morocco. In Y. B. Hounet and D. Puccio-Den (eds). *Truth, Intentionality and Evidence* (pp. 126–143). Abingdon, Oxon: Routledge.

Valverde, M. (2015). *Chronotopes of Law: Jurisdiction, Scale and Governance*. Abingdon, Oxon: Routledge.

von Benda-Beckmann, F., von Benda-Beckmann, K. and Griffiths A. (2009). *Spatialising Law: An Anthropological Geography of Law in Society*. Aldershot: Ashgate.

Wendland, W. (2017). The Evolution of the IGC from 2001 to 2016. In P. Roffe and A. Abdel-Latif (eds). *Protecting Traditional Knowledge: The WIPO Intergovernmental Committee on Intellectual Property and Genetic Resources, Traditional Knowledge and Folklore* (pp. 31–54). Abingdon, Oxon: Routledge.

Whatmore, S. (2002). *Hybrid Geographies: Natures Cultures Spaces*. London: SAGE.

World Intellectual Property Organization (WIPO) (2015). Protecting Society and the Environment with a Geographical Indication: Argan Oil Morocco. *WIPO Case Studies*, <https://www.wipo.int/ipadvantage/en/details.jsp?id=2656>.

WIPO (2019). Madrid – The International Trademark System, <https://www.wipo.int/madrid/en/>.

4 The argan producer network and value chains

Comparing different cooperatives and producers

Introduction

With the proliferation of value and commodity chain analyses in recent years, the purpose, methodology, structure, disciplinary focus and written style of these analyses has varied considerably. Many of the early quantitative commodity chain or value chain analyses focus on 'value capture', providing useful insights into the distribution of value-added content and profit at the different stages of the value chain (Gereffi, 1994; 1999). However, it is extremely difficult to gain information from firms on the sale prices of the components they use, and so these studies often rely on estimates of the selling price of that stage's output and subtracting the cost of all purchased inputs (see Dedrick et al., 2008). For cosmetics products, it is often impossible to know the exact quantities specified in individual agreements, such as the cost and value addition at each stage, the cost of research and development (R&D) on specific bioactive ingredients, and even the marketing costs, aside from approximate figures from company annual reports. In addition, these approaches have taken a linear 'chain' approach that is not always in keeping with the reality of the way in which goods and commodities are produced and distributed to numerous buyers and local and international markets, and how they are processed and unprocessed.

Other value chain analyses have a broader political economic focus, with global value chain (GVC) analyses being probably the most predominant (Neilson et al., 2014). This framework provides for analyses that focus on the production, processing, distribution and marketing of specific globally traded products or services, and the main stakeholders involved at each stage (Gereffi, 1994; 1999; Schmitz, 2005; Mather, 2008). These case studies have often been useful for policy-makers and development agencies, for identifying leverage points with a view to improving working conditions, encouraging 'fair trade', encouraging greater value capture at the producer end of the value chain, and identifying environmental and social improvements from the impacts of production and trade (Hughes, 2001; Taylor, 2005; Neilson and Pritchard, 2010). This has been particularly relevant for agri-food and related tropical products, which due to colonial legacies have often been traded simply as raw commodities, meaning minimal income for producers and substantial inequities in the chain (Hughes, 2000; 2001; Dauvergne and Lister, 2011; OECD and WTO, 2013). The United Nations Industrial Development Organization (UNIDO) estimates that developing countries process only 38 percent of their agricultural products, compared to 98 percent in industrialised countries; and the value added of processed agricultural products is 4.5 times less important (in USD/tonne) in developing countries than it is in industrialised ones (UNIDO, 2009; OECD and WTO, 2013).

For the more critical qualitative researchers, analysis of specific commodities or value chains has often been underpinned by the materialist turn in human geography and the social sciences, seeking to understand the co-production of the economic object as commodity, and of its socio-cultural relations (Cook and Crang, 1996; Whatmore and Thorne, 1997; Leslie and Reimer 1999; Cook, 2004; 2011; Hughes and Reimer 2004; Daya, 2014) which Page (2005, p. 293) refers to as 'new geographies of commodities'. As Cook (2004) explains, this research was initially energised by David Harvey's (1990, p. 422) call for radical geographers to 'get behind the veil, the fetishism of the market', and to 'make powerful, important, disturbing connections between Western consumers and the distant strangers whose contributions to their lives were invisible, unnoticed, and largely unappreciated' (Cook, 2004, p. 642). These studies tend to take a useful descriptive narrative approach towards unearthing the distant impacts of trade and production on people and their environments in producer communities. In this book, the value of both approaches is noted, for providing different perspectives about the commodity trade network and also the socio-cultural aspects and impacts on producers making the products in specific geographical places. Therefore, I have separated out these approaches in the following two chapters. This chapter adopts a value-chain type of analysis of 'the bigger picture' that is intended to consider the main influences, flows and impacts of the argan trade and on trade networks. The next chapter (Chapter 5) focuses more on the producers of argan oil and argan products, providing narrative context of the lives of the producers and the more personal impacts on the people, their communities and their environments from the production and trade.

This chapter provides a bespoke value-chain analysis approach, given the various approaches to commodity/value/supply chain network studies. It responds to the call by geographers Leslie and Reimer (1999, p. 404) to 'spatialize' commodity chains, to avoid an excessive focus on the *global* dynamics of production/consumption/retailing linkages, as well as avoiding an overly dualistic and simplistic 'core-periphery' focus that often only superficially examines the reality within 'periphery countries'. It also acknowledges and regularly adopts the language of 'production networks', through which economic geographers have steered away from 'linearity' in chains towards complexity of material relations (Bathelt, 2006) and in 'networks' (as influenced by actor-network theory, see e.g. Law and Hassard, 1999), albeit with contestations over the spatial dimensions of production networks/value chains (Hess and Yeung, 2006; see also Neilson et al., 2014). This chapter adopts a more 'spatialised' or horizontal approach to the analysis of the production network/value chain, particularly with a producer-country end focus, in line with Bolwig and colleagues' (2010) framework, and also with Goodman's (2004) discussion of moral economy in mind. This chapter applies this approach to an analysis of the wider market of agri-food and cosmetic products of Moroccan argan oil (and related products). Bolwig and colleagues (2010) argue for an integration of the 'vertical' and 'horizontal' elements of value chains that affect poverty and sustainability, such that there is a greater focus on the participation of small producers from the Global South in value chains. While this chapter does not fully quantify all of these vertical and horizontal elements, there is at least qualitative information available on the main themes they highlight, plus some existing quantitative evidence from recently sampled communities (Lybbert et al., 2010; 2011; le Polain de Waroux and Lambin, 2013; Huang, 2017). Rather, like most value chain analyses, an analysis of recent historical changes and a snapshot of the current state of various factors is provided. What is more unique in this case, however, is that it is closely focused on producer-end issues and concerns, including value and process 'upgrading' at a local level in Morocco (which is in any case advocated by Bolwig et al., 2010 and Riisgaard et al., 2010). Following this, I then merge into a commodity stories approach (see e.g. Cook, 2004; Daya, 2014) in the next chapter to draw out the narratives that arise from the producer-end issues and concerns.

As discussed in earlier chapters, the specific biological commodity in question is unique. In recent decades, the market for argan has dramatically expanded, as research by Moroccan and foreign researchers has identified the valuable dermatological and hair-care qualities of the oil: it is high in essential fatty acids, and contains polyphenols, tocopherols, sterols, squalene and triterpene alcohols which can have several beneficial effects for the skin, hair and body (Monfalouti et al., 2010). Therefore, much of this analysis focuses on supply of cosmetic argan oil and argan-related skin- and hair-care products.

This chapter continues to focus on the EIG Targanine (producer) cooperatives and their supply chain with BASF Beauty Creations (the cosmetics business arm of BASF, which acquired LS and Cognis) and L'Oréal (including The Body Shop, which was acquired by L'Oréal in 2006 and then sold to Natura in 2017). The NGO Yamana is also involved in this partnership and supply chain, supporting the partners to ensure quality, traceability/transparency, local empowerment and fair pay in Morocco. Importantly, this chapter is also based on interviews with several other businesses and cooperatives which provide a point of comparison against the Targanine–BASF–L'Oréal supply chain. Given the relatively small scale of the industry, and the producer-end focus, this is a more micro-scale production network/value chain analysis than is typical of many other comparable studies of bulk commodities (e.g. Mather, 2008, on bananas, sugar, palm oil and cut flowers; Dauvergne and Lister, 2011, on timber). Nevertheless, this chapter arguably provides useful insights into the structure and effects of the global trade in argan on local producers in Morocco.

Vertical elements: governance and coordination

The use of the word 'chain' implies a typical focus on 'vertical' relationships between buyers and suppliers and the movement of goods and services from producer to consumer.[1] Although the chapter focuses more on the producer end of the argan production network, there are some important factors to consider relating to its trade. Specifically discussed are elements of governance and coordination, which include the effects of lead firms (the focus here is on one specific supply chain as an example), trade rules, development assistance, upgrading and the role of standards in the argan value chain/producer network, before exploring in more detail its effects on the livelihoods of producers – the ultimate concern throughout this analysis.

In 2007–08, it was estimated that approximately 330 tonnes of argan oil were exported from Morocco (CTB, 2010), with the majority destined for Europe, particularly France (more than 160 tonnes), up to over 700–800 tonnes per year in 2012/13 (Boyle, 2013) and then up to 4,000–5,000 tonnes by 2016/17 (Huang, 2017). Although there are not clear figures by use, the majority of the oil exported to Europe is used in cosmetics and hair-care products, with some also used as an alimentary oil. A director of one cooperative member of Targanine (Toudarte) estimated their trade at approximately 80 percent cosmetic and 20 percent alimentary, with the proportion of cosmetic trade expanding (interview, 2011), while other cooperatives put the figure at closer to 60–70 percent cosmetic and 30–40 percent alimentary depending upon whether their trade was mainly local – which led to a higher percentage being used for alimentary purposes – or for export (interviews, September 2014).

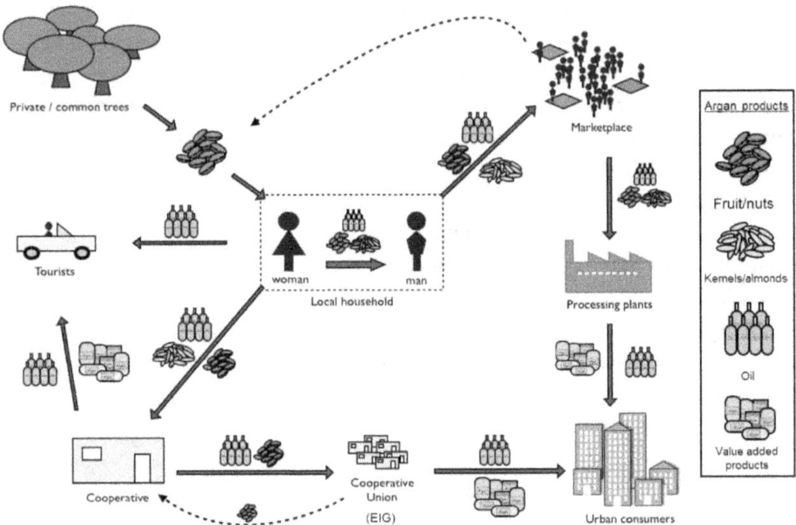

Figure 4.1 The argan commodity network from a producer and household perspective

Source: Adapted from a draft obtained from Yann le Polain de Waroux, as used in le Polain de Waroux (2013, p. 1). Used with Permission.

Argan oil is a high-value oil sold to consumers for about €150 per litre in tourist shops (during fieldwork in 2014, it was sold by cooperatives in small bottles at an average of 150 Dirham or €15 for 100ml) or in bulk at a fair trade minimum price of €23.7 per litre (FLO-Cert, 2014). There are rough estimates that 90 percent of argan oil is exported by private operators, as opposed to 10 percent by the cooperatives (CTB, 2010), despite much of the rhetoric about the contributions of the industry to women's empowerment. To contextualise the network of actors and exchange of components relating to argan, Figure 4.1 provides a basic illustration.

The role of lead firms

The typical starting point for value chain analysis is on the 'lead firms' and their ability to organise activities in a value or supply chain, affecting the division of labour, allocation of resources and distribution of gains. This can include requirements for quality, labelling and certifications, as well as the effects of contracts for purchase of the commodity products. In the case of the argan industry, the trade in argan oil can probably be characterised as buyer-driven, with the boom in the industry largely a result of demand from consumers for cosmetics products, especially in the European Union, but also in the United States and other regions. This means that producer behaviour is to some extent dictated by the regulations and standards set by governments, companies and consumers in these importing regions or countries.

In the Targanine argan supply chain analysed, both BASF and L'Oréal have strongly emphasised quality standards, fair trade and value-addition, and have used a novel product from the supply chain as a kind of 'access and benefit-sharing (ABS)-test case' as discussed in Chapter 3 (see Robinson and Defrenne, 2011). L'Oréal is the lead firm which manufactures and markets a number of skin- and hair-care products containing Targanine-supplied argan oil and other argan plant extracts, including through The Body Shop (owned by L'Oréal from 2006 to 2017). As Charlotte D'Erceville, the argan supply chain project manager for BASF (biochemical testing and supply) has noted, 'the contribution of L'Oréal has been critical to the success of the venture, CSR approach and social fund' (personal correspondence, July 2010). The demand for high-quality products, thereby requiring transparent and hygienic production methods, is evident in this case, to maintain brand image and comply with European and global regulatory quality standards. In addition, these firms have asked for and supported the development of traceability systems which help the Targanine cooperatives maintain three certifications: 'bio' and fair trade, as well as geographical indications (discussed in Chapter 3, and below in relation to standards). The establishment of fair trade payments, as well as benefits for a social fund, have been used as an exemplar case in L'Oréal's 'Solidarity Sourcing' program for socially responsible sourcing of products (which includes an image of a Berber woman holding argan nuts on their website),[2] in an attempt to use value chains as a commercially oriented empowerment tool. Their website notes:

> The proposal of joint sourcing projects in partnership with economic and social experts (NGOs, associations, public stakeholders) thus becomes a major element in the tender decision-making process. Projects are selected and monitored on the basis of a certain number of criteria, including the following: purchasing value, competitiveness in the market, number of jobs created or maintained, reproducibility and sustainability of the project. Solidarity Sourcing projects are thus long-term projects that are essential to the activities of the group and aligned with its purchasing strategy (with regard to quality, competitiveness, lead times, adherence to ethical, environmental and social principles).[3]

These principles include audits of the logistics chain, which were observed during my fieldwork in the presence of BASF and Yamana staff, at the producer end of the chain. Most of these purchasing strategy/Solidarity Sourcing elements were observed, as will be discussed in the following sections.

To provide additional background, a 'corporate socially responsible' supply chain partnership has been developed since 2001, when the beauty care division of Cognis – Laboratoire Sérobiologiques (now part of BASF) – started research on argan oil, as discussed in Chapter 3. Cognis partnered with Professor Zoubida Charrouf and the Targanine cooperatives after the establishment of their economic interest group (EIG) in 2003 to further the business interests of its women's cooperatives. As Turner (2014, p. 217) explains, the GIE/EIGs have specific roles:

> In order to link up cooperative production with the diverse expectations of potential customers, ranging from niche food connoisseurs to the pharmaceutical and cosmetic industries, cooperative marketing networks – known as GIEs (*Groupement d'Intérêt Économique*; Economic Interest Groupings) – have been set up with the support of external partners, with a goal to construct an unbroken commodity chain in which all interest groups are united according to transnational standards. Interwoven into this chain are also national governance institutions.

As I began to explain in Chapter 3, Cognis and Professor Charrouf conducted further R&D on argan products to isolate active ingredients from argan pressed cake (proteins) and argan leaves (flavonoids), with the researchers listed as co-inventors on patents in 2005, 2006 and 2008. L'Oréal then entered the partnership in 2006.[4] A rolling two-year agreement for the supply of argan oil and related products has been established which, due to growth in demand for argan oil in Europe, has meant sustained and expanding purchase of bulk oil from BASF and L'Oréal. This has meant the expansion of the Targanine cooperatives to employment of approximately 557 women across the six cooperatives by the end of 2014 (up to 1,000 women including affiliated women's argan collection centres occasionally supplying the supply chains). The launch of a new range of 'Wild Argan' products by The Body Shop (which, as mentioned above, was acquired by L'Oréal in 2006 and then sold to Natura in 2017), supplied by Targanine through the same supply chain, is also likely to increase the demand and supply of argan given its global presence and volume of sales. At the time of writing (2019), The Body Shop were still selling 'Wild Argan' as sourced from Targanine since 2014.[5]

The payment received by the cooperatives is audited by EcoCert as fair trade certified and this means the bulk of their supply to Europe – estimated at approximately 80 tonnes of oil – is paid at a higher rate than usual: 40 Moroccan Dirham (MAD) or more per kilogram of argan kernel (plus a 5 percent end-of-year fair trade payment), with the benefits going to the cooperatives and women. The supply chain also benefits from being short and generally without 'middlemen-type' intermediaries. Payments follow a simple structure: L'Oréal purchases high-quality chemically tested and validated argan oil from BASF (BASF also sells the product independently), BASF purchases from EIG Targanine (the business unit of the cooperatives) and this money is paid directly to the cooperatives. With the traceability training of Yamana and BASF staff, the account books and ledgers of the cooperative directors are checked annually or more regularly, with women signing when they receive money to ensure that they are paid the appropriate amounts for their work, and money has not been skimmed by intermediaries (interviews, August 2010, April 2011 and September 2014).

These factors combine to have a number of comparable effects against other argan supply chains, regarding both the challenges and advantages that arise from requiring that standards are met and towards producer-end 'upgrading' (discussed below), as well as for the 'horizontal elements' at the producer end of the value chain (discussed in the second half of this chapter, and continued in Chapter 5). Before analysing these issues, I will consider the operation of a number of trade rules and overseas development assistance projects – and their potential effects on argan supply chains.

Trade and aid relevant governance

Outside of the Targanine supply chain are some other 'governance and coordination' factors relating to trade rules or protections, as well as targeted aid relevant to the argan industry and women's cooperatives in particular. Although Bolwig and colleagues (2010) do not specifically discuss these aspects at length in their framework, it is typical to consider them in value chain analyses in general and it would thus be a significant oversight not to do so. Importantly also, Chapter 3, which deals with the legal geography of the argan supply chain, provides additional detail about the trade, intellectual property, indigenous knowledge and access and benefit-sharing laws and frameworks, and the challenges they pose in the argan trade context.

The presence of specific overseas development assistance (ODA) projects led by the European Union's Arganier Project,[6] and also by the German sustainable development implementing agency Deutsche Gesellschaft für Internationale Zusammenarbeit (GIZ – formerly GTZ), has had a significant impact on the argan sector. Both of these projects, with the Moroccan Agence de Développement Social, have helped to create, build and support several women's cooperatives and EIGs to improve rural development and economic growth, women's empowerment and conservation of the argan forest (see Figure 4.2). These have been established so as to ensure the meaningful inclusion of women in the argan industry, whereby

Figure 4.2 Cooperative Taitmatine, which has benefited from foreign aid funding and Foundation Mohammed V Solidarity funding

Source: Taken by the author, Daniel Robinson, 4 August 2010.

they contribute to decision-making and also benefit from the expanded demand for argan. This is set against the backdrop of many shop-front sales businesses established to capitalise on this demand, which have sometimes been criticised for undertaking unscrupulous activities (e.g. poorly paying staff, including women, for mixing argan with other oils, and for claiming Souss Valley regional origin when in fact they are made in other parts of Morocco, like the surrounds of Casablanca or Marrakech). The presence of these agencies has arguably helped to improve the rural development prospects of many regional communities and has also meant the direction of funding to legitimate cooperatives to purchase machinery or gain certifications which give them a market advantage (as noted in some interviews with producers).

Given that the European Union is Morocco's largest trading partner, with total trade worth €27 billion between the country and the region in 2013, there are a number of relevant agreements in place. The current framework for trade was put in place in 2000 and is an Association Agreement establishing a free trade area of gradual trade liberalisation and expansion of market access, covering certain goods and with longer lead-in periods for Morocco. This is being superseded by negotiations for a Deep and Comprehensive Free Trade Area (DCFTA) between the European Union and Morocco, which started in March 2013 with the intent of bringing Moroccan legislation closer to that of the European Union. The purpose of the negotiations is to expand the terms of the existing Association Agreement to include trade in services, procurement, competition, intellectual property rights and investment protection, as well as areas like industrial standards and sanitary and phytosanitary measures.[7] Of particular relevance here is the EU–Morocco Agreement on Agricultural, Processed Agricultural and Fisheries Products, which entered into force in October 2012. According to European Union fact sheets, the agricultural agreement means that 98 percent of Moroccan agricultural products sold as exports to the European Union can have access to European markets with a duty of 0 percent immediately, and with delayed liberalisation of Moroccan duties for European Union products entering Morocco. Also included in the agreement are ongoing commitments towards negotiations to an agreement on the protection of geographical indications (explicitly mentioning recognition and protection of argan oil as a purely Moroccan product) (Reviron and El Benni, 2012).[8] However, the potential advantage of liberalised markets for products such as argan oil in Europe is tempered by the higher expectations for sanitary and phytosanitary standards being negotiated and introduced. For example, the Moroccan and French governments have recently signed an agricultural agreement for sanitary and phytosanitary cooperation on 10 February 2014, ahead of higher expectations from Europe for food and related products, including cosmetics, coming from Morocco (discussed further below in relation to standards).[9] Morocco is also a WTO member and thus has to comply with the sanitary and phytosanitary measures (SPS Agreement) outlined by the WTO, albeit focused on trade-related SPS measures (e.g. avoiding trade discrimination, and promoting transparent science-based risk assessment). The SPS Agreement provides longer timeframes for compliance on products of interest to developing country WTO members so as to maintain opportunities for their exports (article 10). However, these timeframes are often shortened through bilateral agreements as countries like Morocco seek to expand their export markets in developed countries.

Value chain upgrading

Upgrading typically refers to a process whereby firms or entire sectors take on more complex and profitable production functions within a value chain. It may also refer to firms adding more value to products with a view to capturing more value in the chain (Mather, 2008). In the context of the argan industry, incremental upgrading in Morocco has been the most common process, with relatively few business actors able to produce whole high quality, cosmetic products for export and sale in Europe. Bolwig and colleagues (2010) note four main types of 'upgrading' of the value chain for a specific commodity:

- process upgrading – usually of equipment to create more efficient production of direct benefit to the producers (see also Humphrey and Schmitz, 2002);
- product upgrading – moving into products with increased unit value;
- functional upgrading – increasing the skill content of the producers; and
- inter-chain upgrading – applying competencies acquired in one function to a different sector/chain.

Specific to the Targnine–BASF–L'Oréal supply chain are noticeable elements of upgrading related to each of these:

- Process upgrading – including investment in equipment by the Targanine cooperatives using income derived from their fair trade annual payments, profit margins and grants received from Moroccan and European agencies and donors. These have been used to purchase improved oil filtration units and mechanical presses (allows faster filtration and pressing of argan kernels and hence faster supply of oil to the market), as well as 'de-pulpage' machines which strip fruit of their husks, allowing women to focus on aspects of their labour that are income-producing (i.e. cracking argan nuts).

- Product upgrading – in this case, through the sale of the by-product of the oil from which a protein is extracted, the Targanine cooperative has the added advantage over other cooperatives of being the exclusive supplier of this 'pressed cake' and thus is the recipient of benefits to a social fund. In addition, Targanine, much like other cooperatives in the region, has developed lines of several different packaged oils, soaps, skin creams and related argan goods. These are mainly sold to local markets, tourists and, in some cases, exported in small quantities.
- Functional upgrading – increasing the skill content of the women by training them to do filtration and basic QA/QC in laboratories based in the cooperatives. This has allowed them to keep their contract with BASF to date, which requires a level of quality and hygiene standards. Although in some of the Targanine cooperatives women are employed to do this work, other cooperatives have put men on salary to be the technical and laboratory managers and to maintain the equipment.
- Inter-chain upgrading – the women and cooperatives now also produce their own alternative products using the same machinery and the cosmetics/skin/hair-care training they have received (e.g. almond nut oil, nigella sativa creams and shampoos, and cactus oil products), which goes beyond just the argan products noted above and increases revenues for the cooperatives.

In addition, there are other elements of upgrading that can be considered. For example, the growing demand for wholesale argan oil combined with having two-year fixed contracts arguably gives greater security and reduces risk for the Targanine cooperatives and women in the medium term. Receiving better pay from BASF for the same product (under fair trade conditions and due to the quality of the oil) might also be considered a minor 'upgrading' element in the value chain. All other cooperatives had irregular but increasing demand with few fixed contracts, and generally received lower average pay per kilo of kernel (and per day/month).

For comparison, there was relatively little upgrading taking place in the other cooperatives that were interviewed, with the exception of mechanical process upgrading in some cooperatives like Tighanimine in Drargha, 10 kilometres from Agadir (provided by the German Embassy). Others such as the UCFA cooperatives (of which there are 22, with a total of 1,000 women members, and with groups at four of these cooperatives interviewed) remain deliberately non-mechanical, preferring to hand-press the oil as has been done traditionally with a stone wheel. This means that their rate of oil production is typically much slower, but the likely lesser volume sold is traded off against the women's preference to use traditional production processes. Many cooperatives, including UCFA and Tighanimine, were pursuing product upgrading for their own sales to tourists, as exports and in local markets, particularly soaps, bottled alimentary oils and some creams and shampoos. While this kind of product upgrading does not really build 'vertical linkages' in existing value chains, the products may be used to enter into new markets (e.g. tourists, hammams and online sales), creating additional revenue for the women at the cooperatives.

Effect of standards

The monitoring of foreign regulatory standards of traded goods by the European Union and other developed countries is evident in reports such as that written by van Wagenberg and colleagues (2012) and can affect the ability of developing country producers to export and join value chains. This sort of comparative analysis of food, environment, labour and non-trade standards (as relating to traded goods) can be used to leverage higher standards through trade agreements (one of the key recommendations of this report to the European Union), increasing the challenges for regulators, businesses and producers in countries like Morocco. On food safety, for example, van Wagenberg and colleagues (2012, p. 34) note in relation to Morocco that:

> New food safety legislation was implemented with Loi no. 28-07 '*relative à la sécurité sanitaire des produits alimentaires*' in February 2010. It prescribes [food business operators] *fbos* to use self-control systems for food safety authorised by the competent authority, establishes traceability throughout the entire supply chain and requires farmers to record the use of fertilizers and pesticides . . . In 2010, Morocco also established a national food safety authority, '*Office National de Sécurité Sanitaire des Produits Alimentaires*' (ONSSA) with law n° 25-08 . . . Currently, the official export control programs, the auto-controls of *fbos* and the traceability systems in place at pack houses generally provide assurance that food of plant origin exported to the EU complies with EU legal limits for pesticide residues. However, exporters and farmers in Morocco are not always sufficiently aware that some of the plant protection products authorised in Morocco are not allowed in the EU and that the lack of *maximum residue levels* (MRLs) in Morocco can lead to residues above EU MRLs.
>
> [emphasis in the original]

This has led to traceability programs implemented by argan-producing cooperatives, often with ODA from Europe, towards 'bio' certification for cooperatives where low levels of or nil pesticides are used. This goes beyond just alimentary oils and includes measures to ensure cosmetics and related skin- and hair-care products do not contain harmful ingredients. The European Regulation (EC) No. 1223/2009 on Cosmetic Products, for example, has strict rules on traceability throughout the supply chain, with customs often depicted as a bottleneck. It annexes toxic or potentially harmful substances as having banned or restricted uses, including phthalates, which have been known to be found as a by-product of the filtration process in argan oil production if not properly controlled (e.g. using non-phthalate plastics).[10]

This has led to training and support from BASF and Yamana at the Targanine cooperatives, GIZ training and provision of specific equipment from 'Project Arganier' to Targanine and Tighanimine. For example, Tighanimine had a machine that is Moroccan-made, but funded by the German Embassy, which filters the oil without any plastic, thus avoiding potential contamination: 'Most use plastic filters – this is the only machine in the region that we know of that filters the oil like this' (interview, 16 September 2014). They also produced cosmetics in bottles and creams and soaps, with training from a Dutch company, but had only been exporting these in small quantities to date because the European Union standards would require testing for larger quantities of exports for European distribution, and so most of their exports are of bulk oil (as is the same for Targanine) (interviews, 15 and 16 September 2014).

Consumer expectations have also driven non-regulatory standards through certifications. The regulatory standards for food and cosmetics have encouraged 'bio' certifications, which have been in place for alimentary and cosmetic oils for several years at Targanine and at UCFA, and at Tighanimine and Tirit d'Argan since 2012. For smaller and newer cooperatives, it was evident that they had found it difficult to meet these standards, requiring time to establish traceability processes and record-keeping (interviews, 17 September 2014).

Similar requirements exist for GI protection, for which the argan fruit must be collected and labelled from specific districts in the region to guarantee its origins and quality. For those who want to have their products distinctly recognised, they are required to ensure proper traceability processes, record-keeping and pay the costs of certification. In doing this, they weigh the costs against the potential benefits of higher payments for oil than other products on the market – but there is a risk in doing so, unless consumers are sufficiently informed about these aspects of the process.

The other important certification standard for the argan industry is fair trade. Depending upon the certification scheme, this typically requires a fixed minimum purchase price (e.g. FLO-Cert), or it specifies that an additional 5–10 percent is paid on top of a bulk purchase (e.g. EcoCert). Certain minimum standards or codes of conduct are also typically set – for example, ensuring that there is no exploitative child labour involved and there are safe conditions to work in, as well as limited and defined working hours. While several of the argan cooperatives were certified according to different fair trade schemes, it was notable from interviews with businesses, shop vendors and some smaller cooperatives that only relatively few producers from the argan industry – typically cooperatives – have achieved this status (interviews, 15–17 September 2014). As will be discussed below, it is mainly those women's cooperatives that have successfully entered into partnerships opening up their trade into global value chains or those cooperatives that have received some targeted ODA (e.g. purchase of machinery, facilities or buildings) that have achieved a more than marginal improvement to livelihoods and income.

Horizontal/distributional producer network elements

The preceding discussion has focused predominantly on the vertical links and chains related to argan commodities emphasising downstream effects from networks of exchange, consumption and regulations and standards at this end. Value chain and global production network analyses have increasingly become interested in understanding the possible effects of trade linkages on poverty and inequality. Bolwig and colleagues (2010) encourage an expanded horizontal analysis of the ways in which the impacts, and nature, of integration into globalised systems are locally mediated (see Goodman and Watts, 1994; Goodman, 2004). Arguably, an expanded focus on the micro-scale impacts and issues for producers is illuminating and important for understanding local poverty, inequality and labour (Barrientos, 2007; Neilson and Pritchard, 2010). As supported by existing studies of the effects of the argan industry through household surveys (Lybbert et al., 2010; Lybbert et al., 2011; le Polain de Waroux and Lambin, 2013) from geography and development economics literature, this study focused specifically on the livelihood effects for the women's cooperatives and their families vis-à-vis argan businesses. Acknowledging the criticisms of analyses that focus entirely on poverty in terms of income and basic needs, Chapter 5 addresses aspects of 'desire' and the more human aspects (e.g. cultural, familial and personal revelations) in the argan industry.

To explore the local livelihoods implications, including issues of power relations, participation, gender and environment, this chapter adopts several of the elements highlighted by Bolwig and colleagues (2010) and other production network authors (Coe, 2012) as points for analysis at the production 'node'. Here, comparisons between producer-end actors are made (i.e. cooperatives, associations, businesses).

Terms of participation

The inclusion or exclusion from participation in supply to a particular market, and also the pre-conditions and terms of participation, reveal much about the costs and benefits for producers. For argan cooperatives, the terms of participation were generally presented as positive by the women producers, albeit with some pre-conditions.

In virtually all interviews with women from the Targanine cooperatives, interviewees expressed happiness to be involved in the operation, noting the flexible hours, the importance of the income, the ability to vote on major decisions and the membership-based structure of the cooperatives. To join, they were required to pay 100 Dirham if they joined when the cooperatives were established (e.g. in 2001 at Tagmate). As Targanine has benefited from the booming trade, and especially from its supply chains to Europe, the membership fee has gone up dramatically to between 10,000 and 15,000 Dirham. The business manager for GIE Targanine, Latifa, noted in an interview held on 15 September 2014 that they allow the women to pay this off over five years: 'It is just like holding shares. The value can go up. If they leave [the cooperative] they take the money back. If one of the women should die, her family would receive this money.'

In 2011, fieldwork included interviews at 'affiliated centres' to Targanine. These were groups of women producers who were meeting surplus demand, but were not yet part of the Targanine cooperatives – in essence, they were part of a waiting list. It was clear that they were hoping to join the Targanine cooperatives, to enable them to receive the additional fair-trade payments and social fund benefits received (e.g. literacy classes, health-care benefits, sewing equipment and classes, crèches and many other things). For example, at the Targanine cooperative named Toudarte, there were just fewer than 100 women members, with 100 women on a waiting list to join in 2011. At the time, there were approximately 260 women in total in Targanine and this has now increased to 557 at the time of writing (2019), including through the integration of women from these affiliated centres. As explained by the EIG business manager, Latifa, in 2011: 'The cooperatives need to be careful how fast they grow. If they grow too quickly, this is risky for us if the demand from Europe and overseas drops off.'

The terms of participation in this supply chain are highly desirable and in demand, but the opportunity to participate has expanded gradually in recognition of the volatility of global markets. It is also important to note that, since 2011, fair trade payments have been extended to the affiliated centres, where demand had exceeded Targanine's supply of argan oil (personal communication, Charlotte D'Erceville, 15 September 2014). All of the other cooperatives interviewed still had relatively low costs for entry, at approximately 100–150 Dirham, except at Tighanimine. At UCFA, the cost of entry was still low in 2011, meaning their 22 cooperatives had expanded to include 1,000 women. At Tighanimine, the cooperative size was still quite small at 68 women, but the demand to join had risen considerably since the cooperative won a number of awards. The fee to join was 100 Dirham in 2006/07, then went up to 500 Dirham over the course of 2008/10, before rising to 5,000 Dirham now (in 2019) to join – noting that new members are allowed to pay this over a year.

Aside from cost, the main terms of participation involved their role within the cooperatives or argan businesses. Notably, the women in virtually all of the cooperatives interviewed emphasised that they had a say in the decision-making of the cooperatives. This included voting for an air conditioner to make the women more comfortable at the Tighanimine cooperative and voting for a range of different benefits like literacy programs and health care in the Targanine cooperatives. The ability to contribute to investment decisions and be elected to the board of a cooperative were highlighted as key benefits of cooperative membership, by the many interviewees. Several women at UCFA, who were interviewed on 20 December 2011, related this to respect: 'We all listen to each other and accept each other's remarks and suggestions. We're like a big family and there are no secrets.'

Despite these generally positive terms, there were sometimes signs of power imbalances. For example, in several interviews with members from Targanine cooperatives (held during fieldwork in 2011 and 2014), the women noted that they were not used to having any money and so when it came to making investment decisions, they did not know what to say and kept quiet. This might mean that the cooperative presidents (always women voted in by the cooperative) or managers (sometimes men employed on salaries) of the cooperatives could influence investment decisions. Generally, though, these women did not indicate dissatisfaction with these decisions.

Outside of these, some argan businesses and an association were interviewed. These clearly did not have a membership-based structure that allowed voting and participation on relatively level terms. The interviewees avoided answering questions on structure and participation, noting they were just a typical business trying to make money, with the exception of one vendor in the Souk El Had at Agadir, who noted: 'We are like a family too. Like a cooperative . . . We are all men' (interview, 16 September 2014). However, he could not explain how they were similar to a cooperative and some of the staff working at the shop were clearly children of the owner of a school age (approximately 10 and 15 years old). The terms of participation were clearly based on commercial imperatives and opportunism, structured as small patriarchal family businesses, purchasing oil and almonds of families and middlemen in the region for sale to locals and tourists in the markets. The association interviewed was at a family-run argan shop (two women and one man). It had no structure or president like a cooperative, nor was it created by women, and it directly employed salespeople to work in the shop. Furthermore, the women responsible for cracking nuts and pressing argan were paid as members of the association, but did not have the opportunity to vote and had no access to any other benefits (interview, 17 September 2014).

The only other term of participation of note was that the Tighanimine cooperative required the women to have their own land and access to their own trees (as do the UCFA cooperatives, interviews December 2011). The manager there indicated that this was a requirement for fair trade certification (interview, 16 September 2014). She explained that this is for traceability because 'this means the women [and their families] collecting for themselves and avoiding brokers or middlemen selling it to the cooperative at prices that might be higher, after taking a cut for themselves'.

Although this is in itself an admirable attempt to avoid middlemen taking an unnecessary share of payments at the collection and oil production stages, it does potentially raise questions about the exclusion of those that might be the most vulnerable. Landless people are often left with limited access to resources, and Bolwig and colleagues (2010) and Carter and Barrett (2006) note that this type of requirement further contributes to their inability to reach an asset threshold that can assist individuals and families out of 'structural poverty'. As the value of argan trees increased over time, there was evidence from several interviews that people in the greater Agadir region were increasingly enclosing previously communal areas to attain exclusive control over the trees, despite customary usufruct rules (also noted by Lybbert et al., 2011 and Turner, 2012).

Income, poverty and inequality alleviation

While acknowledging the deeply political and moral questions surrounding the conceptualisation of poverty, this chapter focused specifically on the composition of livelihoods and of income and benefits/assets. For understanding the effects of the argan trade on income distribution, there is recent instructive quantitative research by le Polain de Waroux and Lambin (2013), Lybbert, Magnan and Aboudrare (2010), and Lybbert and colleagues (2011) in specific argan oil producing communities. Lybbert and colleagues (2011, p. 13964) note from surveys in Essaouira province that households with access to argan fruit enjoyed higher household consumption relative to other households, more assets in the form of goats, and that girls from these families were more likely to make the transition from primary to secondary school. Similar responses against all of these indicators were also confirmed in the qualitative interviewing we conducted at 14 cooperatives in the greater Agadir region. In the case of le Polain de Waroux and Lambin's (2013, pp. 597–599) study, they note that income in the villages surveyed (near Awluz, close to the city of Taroudant, and near to only one of the cooperatives that I interviewed) was dominated by remittances (averaging 35 percent of total income), farm-related income (31–57 percent of total income), with income from argan much lower, at an average of 4.1 percent of total income, up to about 10–11 percent in some villages. Their analysis of assets also suggested that participation in argan production, including cooperatives, had no significant impact on assets in their study villages. These invoke the suggestion that the argan industry is making only minor impacts on these specific communities. However, they do note that the nominal impact on wealth is due to a number of factors, including: limited raw materials with geographical and temporal variability (noting sparse argan occurrence and dry climate in the surveyed region); market price fluctuations, typically meaning higher oil process in years of scarcity (related to climate) and due to seasonal effects; and entry barriers to the high-quality export market, with private firms appropriating most of the margins from the argan oil trade (le Polain de Waroux and Lambin, 2013). I also note similar findings; however, my fieldwork in relation to several argan cooperatives has an explicit focus on organised production rather than community distribution, making some comparisons impossible.

In the 14 cooperatives interviewed for this chapter, different daily incomes from working in the different cooperatives were noted, with highly variable average income due to differing working hours and productivity between the women, as well as the factors affecting the market noted above by le Polain de Waroux and Lambin (2013). Table 4.1 provides the amounts paid to the women at the time of interview per kilogram of argan kernel, against the approximate daily amount produced, and in some cases estimates of the monthly income. It was often noted that additional income could be earned by collecting and selling fruit at approximately MAD$3–5 per kilogram (in 2014) and MAD$1–2 per kilogram (in 2011) (noting that 10 MAD ~ 1 Euro), or for sale of 'pressed cake' for use in soap at MAD$3 per kilogram for most cooperatives (unlike Targanine, which received a large premium). Some cooperatives with marketable cosmetic products also earned additional income which was either split among the women or used to invest in the cooperative (e.g. Targanine, Tighanimine, Cooperatives A, B and C).

For those women receiving fair trade payments and other quantifiable monetary benefits, they are often able to produce enough to earn MAD$80–85 per day (if they can produce 1 kilogram of kernel, at about €8–8.5 per kilogram). This is above the agricultural minimum wage of 63 Dirham (approximately €6.3) per day (up to 10 hours' work), with the women

Table 4.1 Estimates of income across several argan cooperatives

Cooperative	*Amount (MAD) per kilogram of argan kernel*	*Average kilograms of kernel per day*	*Monthly income estimate per person (MAD)*
Taitmatine	45 (more with inclusions)[i]	1	1,935
Toudarte (Targanine)	40 (85 with inclusions)[i]	1	1,950
Tagmate	40 (more with inclusions)[i]	1	1,800
Tamaynoute	40 (more with inclusions)[i]	1	1,820
Targante	40 (more with inclusions)[i]	1	1,840
Ajdiggue	40 (more with inclusions)[i]	1	1,750
Tighanimine	35 (80 for FT orders)[ii]	0.8–1.5	840–1,575 (up to 1,935)
Cooperative A	30 (FT)	1	900
Association A	40	1.5	1,800 (900)[iii]
Cooperative B	30–40 plus 5–10% FT	1	900–1,200 (up to 1,320)
Cooperative C	30	1	900
Purchase price by middlemen – estimate	15–20	0.5[iv]	225–300

Key:

FT = fair trade

Notes:

(i) Including the fair trade premium payments, other income from sales and the value of the social fund benefits from the pressed cake by-product, which does not involve extra labour from the women (but requires labour from technicians, usually men, paid a separate salary). Some of the social fund benefits may be paid as cash to the women (e.g. at Toudarte) and sometimes this is spent on other benefits and assets, typically shared by the community. Notably, some such as Tamaynout indicated that the price paid is higher if the nuts are from fruit they have collected themselves (in 2011) and that the price varies depending upon climatic factors and market demand.

(ii) Only about 10 percent of orders are currently fair trade, but they also noted some other income from sale of soaps and cosmetics. Sometimes this goes directly to the women; at other times, it has been saved to buy things such as an air-conditioning unit for the cooperative.

(iii) Lack of mechanisation in terms of de-pulpage or mechanical press means the time spent on labour producing kernels is significantly reduced, by an estimate of more than one-half. Hence the 900 figure is more realistic here.

(iv) The middleman price is an estimate based on comments in three interviews at cooperatives and businesses. Here, it is assumed there is lack of mechanisation since our interviews with businesses suggest that the middlemen from whom they purchase buy from families who collect on their own land and surrounds and crack the nuts at home.

having more flexible and typically shorter cooperative working hours – often because of childcare and family responsibilities, themselves forms of unpaid labour. For most cooperatives, however, including some that are certified fair trade, they have a flat rate for oil sales at MAD$30–40 per kilogram, meaning approximately the same amount per day. However, for those cooperatives that do not have de-pulpage machines, this can reduce to MAD$30–40 (€3–4) for approximately two days' work, as the process of removing fruit in order to have argan nuts to crack can be laborious, taking potentially a whole day for a 60-kilogram sack. This is significantly below the agricultural minimum wage. Essentially, this means that there is a significant discrepancy in the income earned by different cooperatives and this therefore highlights the importance of fair trade purchases, as well as investment or ODA grant of machinery on incomes. The significant difference between the estimated price paid by middlemen and the price paid to women by cooperatives (often able to reach export markets) also suggests an advantage in being a member of a cooperative. Notably, the women and managers at UCFA cooperatives expressed a 'per litre' amount for payment of approximately MAD$150 (€15) in 2011, making their income more difficult to compare. Depending upon the amount of rainfall, the size of kernels varies, meaning that somewhere between 3 and 5 kilograms of kernels may be needed to make a litre of oil, suggesting their pay is similar at MAD$30–50 per day (assuming similar speed for the breaking of the nuts). For non-mechanised cooperatives, this amount may be significantly reduced by half (interviews, April and December 2011).

Vulnerability and risk

Many cooperatives had successfully established supply to markets in Europe and domestically that were providing significant incomes and resources. Despite this, these may be sensitive to market volatilities, including market displacement by other cosmetic actives, creating vulnerability and risk, particularly given that several cooperatives indicated that around 80 percent of their production was export-bound. Others, such as Cooperatives A, B and C and Association A, noted some frustration at directly reaching foreign markets, instead being largely dependent on local sales and export sales through intermediaries (thus having a different risk effect based on local markets). Although there are differences among the cooperatives, there were often comments from the managers to the effect that their main frustration and competition was from business:

> There are 5 GIEs of argan in the region in Morocco. We have more competition with companies than cooperatives, because we have a

> higher price than companies. For cooperatives we sell at around 25 Euro per kilogram of oil, but it is more like 19 Euro for companies.
>
> (interview, September 2014)

> . . . We have to explain the quality, the benefits for women and the fair trade aspects. We have to prove certification and improvement of the living conditions of the women. The companies have no traceability. They can't prove any of these things.
>
> (interview, September 2014)

The difference in sales price between certified and non-certified also creates a challenge for the cooperatives that is not unique to argan production. While it provides a quality advantage, it may mean greater sensitivity to the changing demand, currency, prices and climatic trends.

Gender and labour

In an article about the argan trade, Professor Zoubida Charrouf indicated that her initial 16 volunteers for argan cooperative formation in the mid-1990s were all widows and divorcees (Boyle, 2013). Traditionally a woman's activity for consumption at home and sale in local markets, the argan boom has broadened this activity and meant a significant shift in gender–labour dynamics in local communities in the region in a relatively small amount of time. While most interviewees noted that their husbands and families had embraced the additional income and benefits brought by their work in the cooperatives, there were some suggestions that it had caused 'family problems' and even 'divorces' in some cases (interviews, April 2011). But as one manager at Targanine remarked pragmatically: 'If it is a problem for some families, they should not join. They do not have to' (interview, April 2011). From my interviews, despite the acknowledgement that it can be 'hard work that hurts my hands' on a number of occasions (interview 16 September 2014; also December 2011), the women interviewed at 14 cooperatives were almost always positive about its importance for their own well-being. They regularly indicated that the cooperatives provided a support network, particularly in the UCFA, Targanine and Tighanimine cases.

The increasing role of men in the sector was raised repeatedly in interviews, and was generally perceived as contentious, and there was a challenge for me as a researcher and a stranger to encourage the Amazigh women to open up about this issue (see also the discussion about men and 'dodgy cooperatives' in Roberts, 2014). Given the dominant patriarchal cultural effects in Morocco – typically introduced through Arab control, language and culture – it was understandable that the women might not be able to fully explain the shifting gender roles in the argan trade. But as Hoffman (2008) explains, Amazigh women have traditionally had a strong matriarchal role in many parts of Morocco and are crucial to upholding traditions and language, and in terms of their rural and agricultural labour practices. These themes are explored further in Chapter 5.

Environmental awareness and impacts

While a producer-network-wide assessment of environmental impacts (including fuels and transport impacts, packaging and waste) was not possible in this case, there is existing evidence about local land-use change and natural resource management that was confirmed by qualitative evidence from the interviews at the cooperatives, and raised already in Chapter 1. During the interviews, the women almost unanimously indicated that there was strong awareness from the cooperatives and their families and local communities about the need to conserve the trees. This was also generally expressed by those involved in argan sales at small businesses. In the cooperatives, the women noted that damage to trees had been more of a problem in the past, as people tried to dislodge the fruit, cut trees for charcoal and firewood, and allowed their goats to graze during the fruit-collection season (not allowed according to usufruct rules, and the Commissariat for Forests and Water which patrols the forest). But most of the women interviewed suggested that the booming argan trade and the argan cooperatives had a positive effect on forest protection:

> People cutting down trees for wood and fuel was a problem. Before I started working in the cooperative, my own husband used to cut down trees to sell wood at the local market. But now that we have realized that selling oil makes more money, he no longer does it.
>
> (interview, UCFA Cooperative, 11 December 2011)

Several interviewees noted that the main threat to the forest now was from camel herders who brought up truckloads of camels that illegally graze on the forest (see Figure 4.3), as well as clearing for agriculture and drought (although several people believed that the trees were highly resilient to drought and rarely died as a result) (interviews, UCFA cooperatives, 2011; businesses, 2014). In a paper by le Polain de Waroux and Lambin (2011), their surveys in Taroudant province suggest increasing aridity and, to a lesser extent, fuelwood extraction were related to forest decline. From their survey, no effect of grazing by local livestock was found. During my fieldwork, several interviewees did note that there were some people in other villages still ignorant and damaging the forest. Despite this awareness, the

Figure 4.3 A herd of camels brought to graze near Imsouane, Morocco

Source: Taken by the author, Daniel Robinson, 17 September 2014.

existence of continued degradation is supported by Lybbert, Magnan and Aboudrare (2010, pp. 13964–13965), who suggest that booming argan markets have not improved the argan forest at a macro scale, using analysis of remotely sensed data from the 1980s until 2009, particularly in the northern part of the region towards Essaouira.

Summary

By adopting some of the key sustainable and fair production themes typical of the global production network/global value chain literature (Bolwig et al., 2010; Coe, 2012; Neilson et al., 2014), this chapter has helped to both quantitatively (where data is available) and qualitatively characterise the effects of the argan trade, particularly on the production end of the network and value chain. There were clear benefits for the women who had been able to join the cooperatives, in terms of income, assets, capabilities and well-being. The cooperatives that had been most successful at providing higher incomes and benefits to their women members had been those that had established export agreements with companies, received training related to quality and towards certifications, and had received grants and ODA towards machinery which saved labour, improved quality and allowed for some basic upgrading into argan product value chains. As explained in Chapter 3, and quantified here, the benefit-sharing agreement for argan 'pressed cake' significantly improved the number and regularity of social/well-being benefits to the members of the Targanine cooperatives, while fair trade and 'bio' certifications had typically assisted the cooperatives in attaining contracts for export to Europe and flow-on benefits. On the other hand, some cooperatives such as Cooperatives A and C particularly, noted the challenges in obtaining certification to prove the quality of their product – because they had to compete with businesses that undercut their price locally for local sale to tourists and for potential exports. Although the activities of the cooperatives have arguably resulted in gradual changes towards women's empowerment (in line with the way in which the production is marketed), it is clear that their freedoms are still limited by systemic patriarchal effects on women, the Amazigh people and, especially, Amazigh women. With these issues in mind, Chapter 5 explores in more detail the lives of the producers working in the cooperatives, against the backdrop of evolving liberties and rights of (Amazigh) women in Morocco.

Notes

1 I acknowledge the inherent flaw in using the terms 'vertical' and 'horizontal' here; indeed, the linearity of the chain can be questioned. In this case, a commodity 'circuit' can be imagined in the way The Body Shop appeals to the Berber tradition of argan oil use as a way of marketing the site of production to consumers in shops predominantly in places like Europe, the United States of America, Canada and Australia, thus realising a circuit of co-production.

2 There is a slight contradiction in this image, as the Berber woman has henna drawn on her hands in which she holds the argan nuts – this practice is not permitted when cracking nuts, because the henna may contaminate the kernels (interviews, September 2014). The marketing does not always quite match the realities of production for the Amazigh women.

3 For more information, see the L'Oréal website: <http://www.loreal.com/suppliers/our-sustainable-procurement-policy/socially-responsible-purchasing.aspx>.

4 L'Oréal website, 'Sharing Beauty with All', <http://www.loreal.com/csr-commitments/sharing-beauty-with-all.aspx> and <http://www.loreal.com/sharing-beauty-with-all/developing-sustainably/solidarity-sourcing-purchasing-as-a-lever-for-social-inclusion.aspx> accessed 15 October 2014.

5 For more information, see The Body Shop's information regarding 'Community Trade Organic Argan Oil from Morocco': <https://www.thebodyshop.com/en-au/ingredient/argan-new>.

6 For more information on this, see: <https://ec.europa.eu/commission/presscorner/detail/en/IP_02_1685> and <http://ec.europa.eu/europeaid/documents/case-studies/morocco_femme_fr.pdf>.
7 For more information, see <http://ec.europa.eu/trade/policy/countries-and-regions/countries/morocco/>.
8 For more information, see <https://eeas.europa.eu/delegations/morocco/4347/morocco-and-eu_en>.
9 For more information, see <http://www.maroc.ma/en/news/morocco-france-sign-three-agreements-sanitary-phytosanitary-and-agricultural-training-fields>.
10 For more information, see <http://europa.eu/legislation_summaries/consumers/product_labelling_and_packaging/co0013_en.htm>.

References

Barrientos, S. (2007). Global Production Systems and Decent Work. Working Paper 77. Geneva: International Labour Office, Policy Integration Department.

Bathelt, H. (2006). Geographies of Production: Growth Regimes in Spatial Perspectives – Toward a Relational View of Economic Action and Policy. *Progress in Human Geography*, 30(2), pp. 223–236.

Bolwig, S., Ponte, S., du Toit, A., Riisgaard, L. and Halberg, N. (2010). Integrating Poverty and Environmental Concerns into Value-Chain Analysis: A Conceptual Framework. *Development Policy Review*, 28(2), pp. 173–194.

Boyle, M. (2013, 1 July). Liquid Gold for Hair Entices Ex-Goldman Analyst, L'Oréal. *Bloomberg Business*, <http://www.bloomberg.com/news/2013-06-30/argan-oil-gives-beauty-boost-to-l-oreal-unilever-redken.html>.

Carter, M. R. and Barrett, C. (2006). The Economics of Poverty Traps and Persistent Poverty: An Asset-Based Approach. *Journal of Development Studies*, 42(2), pp. 178–199.

Coe, N. (2012). Geographies of Production II: A Global Production Network A–Z. *Progress in Human Geography*, 36(3), pp. 389–402.

Cook, I. and Crang, P. (1996). The World on a Plate; Culinary Culture, Displacement and Geographical Knowledges. *Journal of Material Culture*, 1(2), pp. 131–153.

Cook, I. (2004). Follow the Thing: Papaya. *Antipode*, 36(4), pp. 642–664.

Cook, I. (2011). Geographies of Food: Afters. *Progress in Human Geography*, 35(1), pp. 104–120.

Dauvergne, P. and Lister, J. (2011). *Timber*. Cambridge: Polity Press.

Daya, S. (2014). Beyond Exploitation/Empowerment: Re-imagining Southern Producers in Commodity Stories. *Social and Cultural Geography*, 15(7), pp. 812–833.

Dedrick, J., Kraemer, K. and Linden, G. (2008). Who Profits from Innovation in Global Value Chains? A Study of the iPod and Notebook PCs. Sloan Industry Studies Annual Conference. Boston, Massachusetts.

FLO-Cert (2014). Fairtrade Minimum Prices and Premiums, <http://www.fairtrade.net/price-and-premium-info.html>.

Gereffi, G. (1994). The Organization of Buyer-Driven Global Commodity Chains: How United States Retailers Shape Overseas Production Networks. In G. Gereffi and

M. Korzeniewicz (eds). *Commodity Chains and Global Capitalism* (pp. 95–122). Westport, Connecticut: Praeger.

Gereffi, G. (1999). International Trade and Industrial Upgrading in the Apparel Commodity Chain. *Journal of International Economics*, 48(1), pp. 37–70.

Goodman, D. and Watts, M. (1994). Reconfiguring the Rural or Fording the Divide? Capitalist Restructuring and the Global Agro-Food System. *Journal of Peasant Studies*, 22(1), pp. 1–49.

Goodman, M. K. (2004). Reading Fair Trade: Political Ecological Imaginary and the Moral Economy of Fair Trade Foods. *Political Geography*, 23(7), 891–915.

Harvey, D. (1990). Between Space and Time: Reflections on the Geographical Imagination. *Annals of the Association of American Geographers*, 80(3), pp. 418–434.

Hess, M. and Yeung, H. (2006). Whither Global Production Networks in Economic Geography? Past, Present, and Future. *Environment and Planning A*, 38(7), pp. 1193–1204.

Hoffman, K. E. (2008). *We Share Walls: Language, Land, and Gender in Berber Morocco*. Oxford: Blackwell.

Huang, P. (2017). Liquid Gold: Berber Women and the Argan Oil Co-operatives in Morocco. *International Journal of Intangible Heritage*, 12(1), pp. 140–155.

Hughes, A. (2000). Retailers, Knowledges and Changing Commodity Networks: The Case of the Cut Flower Trade. *Geoforum*, 31(2), pp. 175–190.

Hughes, A. (2001). Global Commodity Networks, Ethical Trade and Governmentality: Organizing Business Responsibility in the Kenyan Cut Flower Industry. *Transactions of the Institute of British Geographers*, 26(4), pp. 390–406.

Hughes, A. and Reimer, S. (2004). *Geographies of Commodity Chains*. London: Routledge.

Humphrey, J. and Schmitz, H. (2002). Developing Country Firms in the World Economy: Governance and Upgrading in Global Value Chains. INEF Report 61/2002. University of Duisburg, Essen.

Law, J. and Hassard, J. (eds). (1999). *Actor Network Theory and After*. Oxford: Blackwell.

le Polain de Waroux, Y. (2013). The Social and Environmental Context of Argan Oil Production. *Natural Product Communications*, 8(1), pp. 1–4.

le Polain de Waroux, Y. and Lambin, E. (2011). Monitoring Degradation in Arid and Semi-Arid Forests and Woodlands: The Case of the Argan Woodlands (Morocco). *Applied Geography*, 32(2), pp. 777–786.

le Polain de Waroux, Y. and Lambin, E. (2013). Niche Commodities and Rural Poverty Alleviation: Contextualizing the Contribution of Argan Oil to Rural Livelihoods in Morocco. *Annals of the Association of American Geographers*, 103(3), pp. 589–607.

Leslie, D. and Reimer, S. (1999). Spatializing Commodity Chains. Progress in Human Geography, 23(3), pp. 401–420.

Lybbert, T., Aboudrare, A., Chaloud, D., Magnan, N. and Nash, M. (2011). Booming Markets for Moroccan Argan Oil Appear to Benefit Some Rural Households While Threatening the Endemic Argan Forest. *Proceedings of the National Academy of Sciences*, 108(34), pp. 13963–13968.

Lybbert, T., Magnan, N. and Aboudrare, A. (2010). Household and Local Forest Impacts of Morocco's Argan Oil Bonanza. *Environment and Development Economics*, 15(4), pp. 439–464.

Mather, C. (2008). Value Chains and Tropical Products in a Changing Global Trade Regime. Issue Paper No. 13. Geneva: International Centre for Trade and Sustainable Development.

Monfalouti, H., Guillaume, D., Denhez, C. and Charrouf, Z. (2010). Therapeutic Potential of Argan oil: A Review. *Journal of Pharmacy and Pharmacology*, 62(12), pp. 1669–1675.

Neilson, J. and Pritchard, B. (2010). Fairness and Ethicality in Their Place: The Regional Dynamics of Fair Trade and Ethical Sourcing Agendas in the Plantation Districts of South India. *Environment and Planning A*, 42(8), pp. 1833–1851.

Neilson, J., Pritchard, B. and Yeung, H. (2014). Global Value Chains and Global Production Networks in the Changing International Political Economy: An Introduction. *Review of International Political Economy*, 21(1), pp. 1–8.

Organization for Economic Development and World Trade Organization (OECD and WTO) (2013). *Aid for Trade and Value Chains in Agrifood*. Geneva and Paris: WTO and OECD.

Page, B. (2005). Paying for Water and the Geography of Commodities. *Transactions of the Institute of British Geographers*, 30(3), pp. 293–306.

Reviron, S. and El Benni, N. (2012). Morocco: Argan Oil. In M. Blakeney, T. Coulet, G. Mengistie and M. Tonye Mahop (eds). *Extending the Protection of Geographical Indications: Case Studies of Agricultural Products in Africa* (pp. 255–265). Abingdon, Oxon: Earthscan/Routledge.

Riisgaard, L., Bolwig, S., Ponte, S., Du Toit, A., Halberg, N. and Matose, F. (2010). Integrating Poverty and Environmental Concerns into Value-Chain Analysis: A Strategic Framework and Practical Guide. *Development Policy Review*, 28(2), pp. 195–216.

Roberts, N. (2014, 13 July). A Moroccan Entrepreneur Brings Argan Oil to America by Way of Women's Co-ops. *The Guardian*, <https://www.theguardian.com/money/2014/jul/13/argan-oil-morocco-entrepreneur-skin-hair-cosmetics>.

Robinson, D. and Defrenne, E. (2011). *Argan: A Case Study on ABS*. Amsterdam: Union for Ethical Biotrade.

Schmitz, H. (2005). *Value Chain Analysis for Policy-Makers and Practitioners*. Geneva: International Labour Organization.

Taylor, P. (2005). In the Market But Not of It: Fair Trade Coffee and Forest Stewardship Council Certification as Market-Based Social Change. *World Development*, 33(1), pp. 129–147.

Trade for Development Centre (CTB) (2010). *Huile d'argan? L'or du Maroc?* Brussels: Agence Belge de Développement.

Turner, B. (2012). Intervention transnationale et moralisation de la gestion de la propriété en milieu rural au Maroc. *Anthropologica*, 51(1), pp. 1–14.

Turner, B. (2014). Neoliberal Politics of Resource Extraction: Moroccan Argan Oil. *Forum for Development Studies*, 41(2), pp. 207–232.

UNIDO (2009). *Industrial Development Report 2009: The Role of Technology and Innovation in Inclusive and Sustainable Industrial Development*. Vienna: UNIDO.

van Wagenberg, C. P. A., Brouwer, F. M., Hoste, R. and Rau, M. L. (2012). *Comparative Analysis of EU Standards in Food Safety, Environment, Animal Welfare, and Other Non-Trade Concerns with Some Selected Countries*. Brussels: European Parliament.

Whatmore, S. and Thorne, L. (1997). Nourishing Networks: Alternative Geographies of Food. In D. Goodman and M. Watts (eds). *Globalising Food: Agrarian Questions and Global Restructuring* (pp. 211–224). Abingdon, Oxon: Routledge.

5 Women's producer stories, solidarity and empowerment

Introduction

While the value-chain approach adopted in Chapter 4 has been useful for comparing the effects of the argan trade between different supply chains, the voices of local producers in typical 'global value chain' analyses are often unheard, or otherwise represent only a fraction of the reporting. The result is a somewhat 'de-humanised' analysis of economic 'development-oriented' factors, and an 'overview' perspective is portrayed, even if a more 'spatialised' approach is undertaken (Leslie and Reimer, 1999) – or even if there is an emphasis on production networks rather than linear chains (see Page, 2005; Bathelt, 2006), like in Chapter 4. Therefore, it is incredibly important to convey some of the stories of the Amazigh women producers themselves – and the way in which they see some of the benefits and impacts of the argan trade – through more qualitative narratives. This chapter will therefore explore some of these narratives, in line with Cook's (2004; 2006) 'following the stuff' approach to thinking about commodity production networks, through a deeper analysis of the socio-cultural and economic aspects of producers from the Global South. However, it must first be noted that these commodity stories/geographies of commodities have received some critiques – for example, for focusing too heavily on the consumption end – as the main site for re-materialisation of social relations and cultural meaning by 'removing of the veil' of the commodity (Harvey, 1990; Daya, 2014). As Daya (2014, p. 813) explains, these commodity story accounts have important moral and political intentions, but she argues that 'producers in the Global South, in particular, are imagined primarily in developmental terms, such that the literature gives little sense of Southern producers as more than economic actors, narrowly defined'. While global value chain and commodity story approaches typically foreground the agency of producers and emphasise the livelihood-based struggles and exploitations that occur in the context of the linkages between local production and global markets, the lens of empowerment and agency also often retains a narrow focus on the economic realm, thus circumscribing the identity of producers (see Goodman, 2004; Daya, 2014). The 'ordinary' stories, or ordinary parts of the lives and social relations of Southern producers – particularly African producers – are seldom told (Edjabe and Pieterse, 2010). Despite this observation, Miller (2010, p. 135) encourages researchers to consider the mutuality inherent within the process of making material goods and products, which is as much about 'things making people as much as people mak[ing] things'.

Here, we find Shari Daya's (2014, p. 814) paper particularly poignant, with her stories of South African beadwork producers in Cape Town, 'revealing ordinary people whose economic practices are both mundane and socially rich, "materialising" and sustaining such human capacities as love, dignity, memory, friendship and kinship'. Her work shows that production is not only about livelihoods, strategies and struggles, but rather about the creation of both identity and a sense of belonging (Daya, 2014). Carr and Gibson's (2016) 'geographies of making' also encourages us to think about the 'cultures of making' at a range of scales – from the maker's bodily interactions with materials to the industrial region, and beyond. They remind us that 'societies will still need people working with their hands doing somewhat mundane yet skilled things: bricklaying, carpentry, hairdressing, cleaning, mending, and making clothes. Many such tasks cannot be automated' (Carr and Gibson, 2016, p. 310). Even in the seemingly 'mundane' work of production, the material interactions between person and object involves skill and creativity – and these can be very important and sustaining for identity, culture and/or solidarity (see e.g. Ingold, 2010; 2013). The focus in this book on recognising the material conditions of labour, skill and practices, as well as 'human biogeographic' connections to the argan tree and surrounding environment, also align with thinking about the materialities of life in the context of 'new materialism' thinking (Coole and Frost, 2010). 'New materialisms' are a resurgent ontological approach focused on the relational and material connections between people and our world (including 'worldly things', such as the environment/nature or the object of people's labour), in the context of rapid global forces such as technological change and ecological decline (Coole and Frost, 2010).

In this chapter, I consider what it means for Amazigh women to be involved in the cooperatives and the production of argan as it enters this new phase of interest for global markets. I consider the rapid change in income and opportunity for some of the Amazigh women, the different struggles across different cooperatives, and what it means for changing family dynamics and the schooling of Amazigh girls. The insights in this chapter are informed by my fieldwork, through which a total of 14 argan cooperatives were interviewed, including six economic interest group (EIG) Targanine cooperatives, as well as another EIG – L'Union des Coopératives des Femmes pour la production et la commercialisation de l'huile d'Argane (UCFA) – at four cooperative locations, and four other independent argan women's cooperatives. Sometimes, women responded as individuals, sometimes they preferred to discuss as a group, and the managers also generally answered some questions. In addition, six argan shops and businesses (including one association, which was like a family business) were interviewed, to make a point of comparison between the impacts and benefits of argan women's cooperatives on the one hand, and the practices and impacts of the argan businesses and shops on the other (which were mostly run, and fronted, by men), as noted in earlier chapters.

These perspectives are held alongside Hoffman's (2008) explanation of Amazigh women upholding the hard labour of the *tamazirt* – the often idealised (by urban folk) rural farming places such as the argan groves of the Souss Valley. She explains that rural women are expected to uphold 'traditional Moroccan social structure' and to 'channel these traditions and transmit them through female family networks', leading to a feminisation of the Tashelhit language among Amazigh in Southern Morocco (Hoffman, 2008, p. 52; citing Sadiqi, 2003, p. 169). While argan oil production is often hard labour, many Amazigh women who were interviewed suggested that the working conditions and economic outcomes achieved through argan oil production represented a considerable change in their circumstances. The narrative of the hard, rural labour, either supported by or creating Amazigh women's group solidarity and successes, comes out in these interviews. Activities relevant to argan oil production also had the benefit of aligning with existing roles and traditions for the women given their long history of argan use, thus providing a useful continuation of traditional practice for renewed solidarity for the women and for Amazigh culture. I will first explore these themes and then, towards the end of this chapter, discuss them in the context of a recent trend towards more liberal acceptance of women's rights in Morocco (albeit with plenty of scope to advance).

Solidarity and well-being within the cooperatives

One of the key intentions of the book, and particularly this chapter, has been to understand how the Amazigh women's lives might have changed and improved as a result of their involvement in the cooperatives. One of the main themes that arose was the idea of the cooperatives providing a place for 'solidarity' and camaraderie despite many of the other challenges the women faced. Although perhaps over-idealised in the 'exotic' marketing imagery of some of the companies, there were plenty of positive expressions about life as a cooperative member. Throughout my interviews, many of the women expressed their happiness with work in the cooperatives, and the word 'solidarity' was used in most women's cooperatives that we visited: 'It is nice to have all the ladies in this place. You can catch up, talk and gossip. There is sometimes competition between women to produce the most!' (interview, Tagmate, Targanine, September 2014).

There was generally discussion about how the work allowed the women to gather, socialise, talk about their lives and enjoy each other's company. These expressions were particularly strong at the Targanine cooperatives, and the women were often singing together upon our arrival or after we left (although there might have been more 'performance' than usual for our visit). In other cooperatives, there was also spontaneous singing (even when arriving unannounced) and a general sense of well-being in the workplace as reflected in the following quotes:

> The solidarity here is very good – if someone is sick, they all put money together to help them. The women all talk and discuss their problems, give each other advice. They are even so happy they sometimes just break into dance and song.
>
> (Independent certified cooperative, east of Agadir, September 2014)

> It is good to come here – it is a place to socialise, feel solid as a group, help each other with daily concerns. Now they have a lot of money to spend on a lot of different things – food, clothes, furniture.
>
> (Independent certified cooperative, North of Agadir, September 2014)

> We all listen to each other and accept each other's remarks and suggestions [about the running of the cooperative]. We're like a big family and there are no secrets.
>
> (Cooperative member, UCFA cooperative, December 2011)

Many of these discussions also reflected upon the fact that rural life for Amazigh women was hard, and that they had to work hard to support their family and take care of homes, and also farms and land. The interviewees often explained that the cooperatives provided a space where women could talk about their daily lives and their problems, and that this was good for their well-being.

Changes to livelihoods and daily life

At all of the women's argan cooperatives visited, there was some discussion about the significant changes in the women's lives, how important it has been for their family, and how it has affected their income, husbands and children:

> We didn't do anything before working here – we were just at home.
>
> (Cooperative member from Toudarte, EIG Targanine, September 2014)

> Before joining the cooperative, I did nothing. I just made argan oil at home. There was no source of money. Argan oil production now supports the needs of the whole family, my children and husband also. It has improved all conditions of our lives – to buy clothes, food and everything for the children and family. It is not entirely enough but it supports our needs. We can travel to Agadir and to the markets. It is still our only income. My husband is sick, so he stays at home. Everything from here is for the family. I have two daughters who are married and one at home (she works at the cooperative now too). I have three boys as well (six altogether). Two of my boys are married and live outside the town/region. One is still at school. It was hard for me in the past to support the needs of the children. The job helps to send my kids to school. I could not send my son to school without it. Clothes and books and many needs are paid for. So, the job directly supports that.
>
> (Cooperative member, Tagmate, EIG Targanine September 2014)

> I started with nothing. Now I'm more independent, I can take care of my children and their education. Now I own my house, whereas I used to rent, and I no longer have to rely on my husband to get an income.
>
> (Cooperative member, UCFA cooperative, December 2011)

Some of the women were also widows (in three of the interviews), making their work in the cooperatives especially critical for the support of their children:

> I have five children. My husband is dead, so I support the whole family. Before this I was just at home, looking after the home and children. My husband worked the land and then when he died a few years ago,

> the cooperative has been the only source of money. The cooperative has changed my life and the lives of all the women here, and in all the region. Before the families only had their husband's money and this was not enough. I have four boys and one daughter who is married. Of my four boys, there are two out of the village working in another part of Morocco, and two in the village working (not in school). I have two grandchildren who live with my son in Agadir – he is busy driving a car for a living. My other son works here in the village as a manual labourer. Per month I earn 800dh–900. It depends on the quantity I have produced. Sometimes I only get 200dh if I am busy or sick and don't work much.
>
> (Cooperative member, Tagmate, EIG Targanine, September 2014)

These significant changes to the lives of the women, and the way in which the cooperatives enabled greater freedoms, were expressed at *all* of the women's cooperatives interviewed, including independent cooperatives:

> The whole idea of the cooperative is for the women – it is to help local and remote women. Of course, it changes their lives. Usually they just stayed home and now they have money and it helps support their families. They can buy things for their kids and themselves like clothes and toys. The women are mostly from poor families. It also helps remove the pressure from the men in the region – it's good for them too because the men are mainly farmers and it is hard to make a living from that work in this region (due to the desert/drought).
>
> (Cooperative president, cooperative north of Agadir, September 2014)

> [Response from several women in a room of 32 women] Thanks be to God for the change in our lives for the better. It has taken us to places we had never been (other parts of Morocco, like Essaouira, Marrakesh and other cities). Before this we just stayed at home – there was nothing much before, just housework. Some of us produced argan at home and sold it locally [Some other women nod/agree – they did this]. The work here helps the family – it helps them a lot.
>
> (Group of cooperative members, Tighanimine independent certified cooperative east of Agadir, September 2014)

For most interviewees who were women working in cooperatives, the income derived from working there was a substantial part of their overall family income – often the majority. Although not quantified in the same terms as in le Polain de Waroux and Lambin's (2013) study, several women also noted the importance of remittances from family in Agadir and Casablanca (interviews, 2011, 2014). Many women noted their income was higher than that of their husbands (particularly at the Targanine cooperatives). Several women explained how this had improved their attainment of assets, such as white goods, as well as travel within Morocco. Again, this was particularly the case for women from the Targanine cooperatives, as well as the UCFA and Tighanimine cooperatives, where fair-trade payments were typically made at the end of each year by major buyers:

> The first three years [of fair-trade payment] went towards the air conditioning for the crushing room and upstairs where the pressing machines are. Then it has gone to the women. Some payment has been direct to the women and some has been towards feasts that they all come to. Now their focus is to build a crèche. Many women have children and pre-school does not exist here or is not good.
>
> (Tighanimine, independent certified cooperative east of Agadir, September 2014)

> [Question: What do you do with your money?]: Anything we want (laugh)! Go to Agadir, buy clothes for us and the children. Furniture, white goods, fridges and washing machines – we never had these before!
>
> (Toudarte, Targanine cooperatives, September 2014)

The purchase of white goods was explained as highly significant in reducing women's domestic labour and the challenges associated with household care. For example, some women did not have fridges and so fresh food had to be constantly produced and used, and would often spoil. Air conditioning was important for women's comfort, and many cooperatives also bought mats and blankets for women's comfort at work (and also for the home).

Future travel plans were also a common discussion point in the interviews:

> We have helped our families, local people and ourselves. Next, we will go to Mecca!
>
> (Targanine cooperative, September 2014)

> The major benefits are for literacy, training and the travelling we can now afford to do. I could visit Marrakech, Rabat, Casablanca . . . or other places!
>
> (UCFA cooperative, December 2011)

These comments about travelling to cities (including sometimes without the presence of men) is also a matter of excitement for many of the women, given some of the recent freedoms enabled by legal changes that have taken place only in the past 20 years (discussed below) and by now having sufficient income for fuel or transport.

Skills, capabilities and human development

There are also skills, capabilities and well-being outcomes that are not easily measured, and so often forgotten in assessments of poverty impacts. For example, some of the cooperatives such as those at UCFA, Targanine and Tighanimine had invested in literacy and numeracy programs with income derived from 'pressed cake' benefits (in the case of Targanine), from fair-trade payments or sales of product. In interviews at Tagmate (Targanine), UCFA and Tighanimine, the women emphasised the importance of this, because it allowed them to check their payments were accurate and had related flow-on effects for their daily lives. The women also regularly mentioned that incomes and benefits had led to improved health, hygiene and availability of time (e.g. due to use of white goods), improved security of rental/home ownership, improved nutrition, purchase of clothing and blankets, and higher levels of education and happiness:

> Since women have joined, it has helped change the mentality of the women. Now their girls go to school. There is training of the women, numeracy and literacy helps them – this is all new. Before they didn't even know how much they were making in kilograms.
>
> (Interview, independent cooperative North of Agadir, 2014)

> We have a school room in the cooperative, and we have been provided education and training. Our communication skills have been improved/developed – we can write and read a little, and we've had doctors coming to check our health for free.
>
> (UCFA Cooperative, 20 December 2011)

> The most important thing is a bit of literacy. We have a school room in the cooperative, and we have been provided education and training in communication, quality . . . We can now write down our names and read a little.
>
> (UCFA Cooperative, 20 December 2011)

Improved numeracy and ability to read and write in Arabic has important implications for the 'worldliness' of the women, thus enabling them to travel, for example. But it is also important to perform fundamental tasks of relevance to their work and income – such as checking and signing 'the books' to assure that appropriate payment has been made for the amount of nuts cracked or fruit collected. For the purposes of fair trade certification audits, clear bookkeeping is required and the accounts kept by the manager are checked by fair trade organisations like EcoCert or UTZ. With increased general literacy in the cooperatives, there is less chance that a manager or middleman may be taking advantage of the cooperative members or employees, and there is greater independence for the women and cooperatives overall.

The impacts of the Targanine 'social funds' that accrued benefits from the sale of patented L'Oréal products were quite noticeable, where money had been spent on sewing equipment or a crèche for the children. In these Targanine cooperatives, the women had also brought in an optometry clinic, as well as doctors for all of the women, and also bought health insurance for the cooperative members. In other cases, in Targanine cooperatives, the women had not yet decided how to spend their money, as they explained that they were not used to having money to spend (interviews, Targanine cooperatives, September 2014).

Gender in the argan business

The exclusion and inclusion of men in the argan industry is contentious. In a number of media articles and development reports (CTB, 2010; Boyle, 2013; Roberts, 2014), the presence of men is criticised and it is suggested that the cooperatives are not 'real' when men become involved. While several of the cooperatives seemed entirely devoid of men, several others had men working as technicians and in some cases as the business director of the cooperative (while there was always a woman president). As one of the women put it: 'The Director is a man, he is not a member. He has a salary. He coordinates with the government and businesses. It can be hard for a woman to take that role because of travel and the need for assertiveness' (Targanine cooperative, 2011).

Such comments mirror the continuing, albeit declining, patriarchalism present in Moroccan society, and suggest that the empowerment of women generally through the cooperatives has had some important effects (e.g. support networks, income and literacy), while still leaving significant room for improvement in terms of gender equality in society more generally. During my fieldwork, I also visited argan businesses and shopfronts (as opposed to the cooperatives) in the Agadir markets and along roadsides north of Agadir to Essaouira for a point of comparison. Of the several non-cooperative businesses that were interviewed, it was predominantly men who were the managers and salespeople, with women in subordinate roles or not seen at all (interviews, September 2014). As demand for argan oil and argan products has boomed, the number of these businesses has also increased.

Some of the women interviewed at the cooperatives explained that they now earned more than their husbands and that their earnings from the cooperative were a primary source of income for the family. When I asked if this had been a source of household tension, several women at different cooperatives explained that they would only be allowed to join the cooperatives if their husbands were supportive and their family wanted or needed the income. In some of the discussions, women noted that there had been some marital tension and that the proliferation of argan cooperatives might lead to more divorces (interviews, 2011, 2014). It was evident that certain communities were more conservative than others and so there were differences in perspective between the cooperatives about the impacts of the industry on family life (see also le Polain de Waroux and Lambin, 2013).

Family and childcare

For women in many of the interviews held at the cooperatives, it was evident that family and childcare responsibilities compounded other labour-related challenges for women, as discussed above. Despite this, many women were glad to have flexible working hours to help facilitate the pick-up and drop-off of children to school, or they were able to bring their younger children to the cooperatives (Figure 5.1): 'We work from 2 to 5, and it's handy because

Figure 5.1 A playground at one of the Targanine argan cooperatives, Toudarte

Source: Taken by the author, Daniel Robinson, Daniel Robinson, 2 May 2011.

we can take care of our children and the house in the morning' (cooperative member, UCFA cooperative, December 2011).

As noted by Lybbert, Magan and Aboudrare (2010; see also Lybbert et al., 2011), the argan cooperatives appear to have had beneficial effects on the number of children, particularly girls, attending both primary and secondary schools. This was also noted in interviews with the UCFA, Targanine and independent cooperatives, and Cooperative B. Women interviewed across all cooperatives reinforced this point:

> Yes, now we send our children to school, boys and girls. Here in this area we only have a primary school. After, the kids go to Agadir or another larger town for high school.
>
> (UCFA Cooperative 11 December 2011)

> [Question: Do any of your children go to high school?] Yes [three women say yes]. One woman's son is in his third year of high school/college and spends the week in Agadir then comes back on the weekend. She looks after him and pays for him and his things with the help of the work at the coop.
>
> (Group of cooperative members, independent certified cooperative east of Agadir, September 2014)

> The important thing is for the women and daughters that were away in Agadir just doing cleaning jobs to earn some money. Now their daughters are here in the cooperative or in school. It was just some primary school before for their girls, but now it is different. The girls can continue to study.
>
> (Interview, Targanine cooperative, September 2014)

On the day of interviews at an independent certified cooperative, the president had been helping girls find a residence to stay in Agadir to attend college (junior high school), as there was no local college – which is a common problem. She noted:

> There is now a bus coming to take the kids to school, organised by the cooperative. There are 22 boys and three girls going to college in Agadir. It is good that girls are going to school now [and that we can help them]. This will open the door to mean more go to college and high school.
>
> (President, independent certified cooperative east of Agadir, September 2014)

This again highlights that small improvements are being made towards gender equity in terms of opportunities for girls and women. However, in one of the more remote communities that I visited, it was noted by one interviewee that there might be a perverse incentive arising from the argan trade and cooperatives – that families might pull their daughters out of school in order to make money from the production of argan oil (interviews 2014). Most of the larger cooperatives had dealt with this potential problem by having a minimum joining age to enter the cooperatives.

The hard, daily labour

It was noted on several occasions that the work was hard, but worthwhile. It is important to recognise that despites its many benefits the work is not always easy, and that it is physically challenging, exhausting and uncomfortable. These accounts provide a point of difference from the positive portrayals in much of the media and marketing around the argan trade, and are thus important for understanding the human impact of the work, which involves sitting for long periods of time on hard stone floors (usually with mats, blankets and/or cushions to soften the surface – see Figure 5.2), while

Figure 5.2 Blankets and cushions for women to use in the cooperatives or at home

Source: Taken by the author, Daniel Robinson, 2 May 2011.

leaning forward and cracking nuts with a hard stone on a plinth. The women expressed feeling tired, uncomfortable and having sore backs, and commented on the hours and repetitiveness involved in the labour:

> It's hard, but I'm happy. I started with nothing.
>
> (Interview, UCFA cooperative, December 2011)

> Work is really hard, look at my hands! My back is always sore, because of so much sitting down. I have even become a hunchback!
>
> (Interview, UCFA cooperative, December 2011)

The cracking of the argan nuts is hard work, but so can be the collecting of the argan fruits:

> Yes, I like it here, but work is very hard. Not only the nut-breaking, but also collecting of the fruit (I often find snakes . . .). Look at my hand, I have cuts and wounds everywhere.
>
> (Interview, UCFA cooperative, December 2011)

Running the cooperatives also brings many challenges, as expressed by one of the presidents of an independent cooperative that had recently achieved certification:

> Running the cooperative is hard, we are struggling a bit. There is a low amount of argan in the forest because of the drought . . . People are complaining because it is hard to get enough fruit and it is getting more expensive . . . sometimes they buy the fruit from the ladies but occasionally there is not enough cash flow to pay them straight away . . . competing with the sellers in the market is hard too, so we have become certified as fair trade and 'Bio' to explain the quality difference to those other sellers . . . As president, I hardly get any of the money and it has been a difficult market and process (getting certification) in the last three years.
>
> (President, independent certified women's cooperative, north of Agadir, September 2014)

> We have a problem presenting our products and marketing. We have no website [their building is set back from the road and it is not clear they have a shop there]. The signage is not sufficient.
>
> (President, independent certified women's cooperative, north of Agadir, September 2014)

Some of the quality and marketing challenges have clearly been impacted by local businesses who were not selling fair trade or, in some cases, genuine argan oil. In one business north of Agadir, I could see strange-coloured argan oil being displayed and it was explained by several of the women and my translator that this was likely due to argan oil being mixed with inferior oils such as olive oil. When questioned about this, the shopkeeper would not respond to us and said that the manager was not available to answer questions (interview, small business, North of Agadir, September 2014).

Discussion

The argan cooperatives have in many ways rode on the back of a wave of feminism that has swept across parts of Morocco in the last 20 years. Moroccan feminism stands out as a leading case in North Africa and the Middle East following significant activism and reforms since the early 2000s (see Eddouada and Pepicelli, 2010; Skalli, 2011; Salime, 2012). This has seen the 'feminization of Islamist women and the Islamization of the feminist movement' (Salime, 2011, p. xv), in which there is not always a clear secular versus religious binary among feminist activists (Gagliardi, 2019). For two decades, the movement had launched a sustained mobilisation to challenge women's secondary status in family law, *mudawwana* (Salime, 2005; Salime, 2009; Eddouada and Pepicelli, 2010). This movement helped to forge one of the most progressive codifications of women's rights in the region: the 2004 Moroccan Code of the Family institutes gender equality, removes the marital guardian and obedience laws, provides women with the right to initiate divorce and gain custody of children, abolishes repudiation and restricts polygamy (Salime, 2012). Additionally, in 2002, women won 10 percent of parliamentary seats, as an outcome of a long struggle to institute a quota system gained many ministerial, diplomatic and legal positions (Skalli, 2011). Furthermore, in 2007, the Nationality Code was reformed, enabling Moroccan women – not just men – to pass on their nationality to their children.[1] Subsequently, many other codes have also come under scrutiny, such as the penal code after the 2012 suicide of Amina Filali, a 15-year-old woman who was raped and then forced to marry her rapist (Salime, 2012).

For Amazigh women, the challenges are arguably greater than for Arab women, as diverse Indigenous groups struggling to maintain their own traditions and language – despite being estimated to be from 40 percent to as much as 70 percent of the Moroccan population (Symons, 2016; Gagliardi, 2019). In legal reforms, Morocco's 2011 Constitution affirmed the principle of equality between men and women (article 19) and officialised the Amazigh language (article 5) alongside Arabic (Gagliardi, 2019). But despite the many reforms in Morocco for women's and Indigenous rights, there are still reports of resurgent political Islamism, persistent polygamy, underage marriage and impunity for perpetrators of domestic violence – impacting particularly Amazigh women (Symons, 2016; Gagliardi, 2019).

In this context, the development of the argan cooperatives since the early 2000s, and the provision of supports, solidarity and livelihoods, has been an important mechanism for Amazigh women to make improvements to their individual and collective well-being. Professor Zoubida Charrouf, who was instrumental in establishing several cooperatives, including the Targanine cooperatives, explained that this was one of the main purposes of the cooperatives – to support Amazigh women (interview, 2010). Following Daya's (2014) approach, this chapter has reflected upon the importance of the cooperatives for the women's kinship and solidarity, as well as recognising their skill in producing argan oil and the challenges faced by the women and cooperatives, and has given some insight into the 'ordinary' aspects of the lives of the producers.

Although there remain many challenges faced by Amazigh women, the argan cooperative members that were interviewed suggested that these cooperatives were providing incremental benefits towards improved livelihoods, well-being and freedoms for women. As reforms continue to occur in Morocco, the increased opportunity for women and girls to receive further formal education and improve their literacy is likely to increase their capacity to advocate for their rights and to negotiate further freedoms. As a whole, the women's cooperatives do seem to be an important women's empowerment enterprise in the context of the other Amazigh and feminist movements in Morocco and North Africa, and is one space in which Amazigh women are receiving increasing recognition.

Note

1 Dahir no. 1-58-250 du 21 safar 1378 (6 septembre 1958) portant la Code de la nationalité marocaine, <https://www.refworld.org/docid/3ae6b5778.html>.

References

Bathelt, H. (2006). Geographies of Production: Growth Regimes in Spatial Perspective 3 – Toward a Relational View of Economic Action and Policy. *Progress in Human Geography*, 30(2), pp. 223–236.

Boyle, M. (2013, 1 July). Liquid Gold for Hair Entices Ex-Goldman Analyst, L'Oréal, *Bloomberg Business*, <http://www.bloomberg.com/news/2013-06-30/argan-oil-gives-beauty-boost-to-l-oreal-unilever-redken.html>.

Carr, C. and Gibson, C. (2016). Geographies of Making: Rethinking Materials and Skills for Volatile Futures. *Progress in Human Geography*, 40(3), pp. 297–315.

Coole, D. and Frost, S. (2010). Introducing the New Materialisms. In D. Coole and S. Frost (eds). *New Materialisms: Ontology, Agency, and Politics* (pp. 1–43). Durham, North Carolina: Duke University Press.

Cook, I. (2004). Follow the Thing: Papaya. *Antipode*, 36(4), pp. 642–664.

Cook, I. et al. (2006). Geographies of Food: Following. *Progress in Human Geography*, 30(5), pp. 655–666.

CTB (Trade for Development Centre). (2010). *Huile d'argan? L'or du Maroc?* Brussels: Agence Belge de Développement.

Daya, S. (2014). Beyond Exploitation/Empowerment: Re-imagining Southern Producers in Commodity Stories. *Social & Cultural Geography*, 15(7), pp. 812–833.

Eddouada, S. and Pepicelli, R. (2010). Morocco: Towards an 'Islamic State Feminism'. *Critique Internationale*, 46(1), pp. 87–100.

Edjabe, N. and Pieterse, E. (eds) (2010). *African Cities Reader Pan-African Practices*. Cape Town: Vlaeberg and African Centre for Cities.

Gagliardi, S. (2019). Indigenous Peoples' Rights in Morocco: Subaltern Narratives by Amazigh Women. *International Journal of Human Rights*, 23(1–2), pp. 281–296.

Goodman, M. K. (2004). Reading Fair Trade: Political Ecological Imaginary and the Moral Economy of Fair Trade Foods. *Political Geography*, 23(7), pp. 891–915.

Harvey, D. (1990). Between Space and Time: Reflections on the Geographical Imagination. *Annals of the Association of American Geographers*, 80(3), pp. 418–434.

Hoffman, K. (2008). *We Share Walls. Language, Land and Gender in Berber Morocco*. Oxford: Blackwell.

Ingold, T. (2010). The Textility of Making. *Cambridge Journal of Economics*, 34(1), pp. 91–102.

Ingold, T. (2013). *Making: Anthropology, Archaeology, Art and Architecture*. London: Routledge.

le Polain De Waroux, Y. and Lambin, E. F. (2013). Niche Commodities and Rural Poverty Alleviation: Contextualizing the Contribution of Argan Oil to Rural Livelihoods in Morocco. *Annals of the Association of American Geographers*, 103(3), pp. 589–607.

Leslie, D. and Reimer, S. (1999). Spatializing Commodity Chains. *Progress in Human Geography*, 23(3), pp. 401–420.

Lybbert, T., Aboudrare, A., Chaloud, D., Magnan, N. and Nash, M. (2011). Booming Markets for Moroccan Argan Oil Appear to Benefit Some Rural Households While Threatening the Endemic Argan Forest. *Proceedings of the National Academy of Sciences*, 108(34), pp. 13963–13968.

Lybbert, T., Magan, N. and Aboudrare, A. (2010). Household and Local Forest Impacts of Morocco's Argan Oil Bonanza. *Environment and Development Economics*, 15(4), pp. 439–464.

Miller, D. (2010). *Stuff*. Cambridge: Polity Press.

Page, B. (2005). Paying for Water and the Geography of Commodities. *Transactions of the Institute of British Geographers*, 30(3), pp. 293–306.

Roberts, N. (2014, 13 July). A Moroccan Entrepreneur Brings Argan Oil to America by Way of Women's Co-ops. *The Guardian*, <https://www.theguardian.com/money/2014/jul/13/argan-oil-morocco-entrepreneur-skin-hair-cosmetics>.

Sadiqi, F. (2003). *Women, Gender, and Language in Morocco*. Leiden, Netherlands: Brill.

Salime, Z. (2005). *Between Islam and Feminism: New Political Transformations and Movements in Morocco*. PhD thesis. Chicago, Illinois: University of Illinois at Urbana-Champaign.

Salime, Z. (2009). Revisiting the Debate on Family Law in Morocco: Context, Actors and Discourses. In K. M. Cuno and M. Desai (eds). *Gender and Family Laws in a Changing Middle East and South Asia* (pp. 145–162). Syracuse, New York: Syracuse Press.

Salime, Z. (2011). *Between Feminism and Islam: Human Rights and Sharia Law in Morocco*. Minneapolis, Minnesota: University of Minnesota Press.

Salime, Z. (2012). A New Feminism? Gender Dynamics in Morocco's February 20th Movement. *Journal of International Women's Studies*, 13(5), pp. 101–114.

Skalli, H. (2011). Generational Politics and Renewal of Leadership in the Moroccan Women's Movement. *International Feminist Journal of Politics*, 13(3), pp. 329–348.

Symons, E.-K. (2016, 24 March). Morocco's Indigenous Amazigh Women Unite against Islamists and Arab Elites. *Women in the World*, <https://womenintheworld.com/2016/03/24/matriarchal-traditions-in-north-africa-under-threat-from-islamists-and-arab-elites/>.

6 Conclusions

The argan tree and forest represent a highly significant relict species, endemic to Morocco with important arid-zone ecological functions, and with traditional significance to the Amazigh people – especially women – who have used it for close to 1,000 years (or more). The booming interest in argan oil, based on increasing global knowledge about its traditional uses and qualities, has led to a range of changes to rural Moroccan society in and around the Souss Valley, of particular relevance to the Amazigh people. Overwhelmingly, the interviewees in this project have indicated that the argan trade has brought many positive improvements to the livelihoods and well-being of remote Amazigh communities, particularly those women and their families involved in the argan cooperatives.

There is significant evidence of the biocultural significance of the argan forest to the Amazigh people, with archaeological evidence and ethnobotanical texts indicating use in the 11th century or earlier (Ruas et al., 2011; Khallouki et al., 2017), as discussed in Chapters 1 and 2. Some researchers have suggested that there have been agricultural and arboricultural practices that have shaped the growth of the tree over long periods of time (IRD, 2011). Human–plant and 'human bio-geographic' interactions have been occurring for generations, particularly regarding the processing of the oil. The process of cracking the argan nuts is specialised, and the Amazigh women perform this task with expertise. The cracking of the nut is an important tactile skill developed through haptic perception and learning – done incorrectly, the argan kernel will crack and the oil will oxidise. The stone/tool chosen is important and this choice, and the weight of the cracking, relies upon the haptic perception and skill of the Amazigh women. This corporeal interaction between human, object and plant is significant to the ongoing production of quality (unoxidised) oil, and therefore to the livelihoods of the region and the whole regional economy. Through modernisation and technology, unfortunately, what is often being lost is an appreciation of the artisanal craft and skill involved in what may often be seen as manual labour or 'basic tasks'. Carr and Gibson (2016) argue for recognition of a full spectrum of 'making cultures', along with the sensibilities and dispositions that are centred on a deep and considered relationship with materials. This thinking can certainly be extended to the deployment of technical skills with plants like argan, where there is a mutually constitutive interrelation between human and non-humans (Ingold, 2000; 2010; Head et al., 2012). This book has highlighted throughout the importance of the socio-material relationships between Amazigh women and the argan tree and fruit/nuts, as well as recognised the material conditions of labour, skill and practices, aligning with 'new materialism' thinking (Coole and Frost, 2010).

Due to logging, overgrazing and other factors, the argan forest has declined over several decades. In response to both the decline of the forest and its cultural heritage and livelihoods importance, the forest was designated as a United Nations Educational, Scientific and Cultural Organization (UNESCO) Arganeraie Biosphere Reserve in 1998. Alongside this declaration was a successful nomination for, and subsequent registration on, the Representative List of the Intangible Cultural Heritage of Humanity for the 'argan environment, practices and know-how concerning the argan tree' in 2014 (Huang, 2017). This listing specifically highlights the role of Amazigh women and their traditional methods for extracting the oil, their use of the oil, the pharmacopoeia, and the crafting of tools used as part of the cultural heritage listing (UNESCO, 2014; Huang, 2017).

As part of this Arganeraie Biosphere Reserve listing, the Moroccan authorities allow continued customary access and use of argan fruit via seasonal usufruct rights in defined forest tracts called *agdal*. The customary rules have been enhanced with state enforcement for the protection of the forest. As discussed in Chapter 3, at all of the cooperatives that we visited, there was very strong awareness of these laws and, in any case, a strong livelihoods incentive to protect the argan forest for their argan oil production.

Fourteen cooperatives were examined within a value chain/producer network approach and compared in terms of the external factors, such as labelling standards and foreign aid, as well as the many producer-level factors, such as income and terms of participation – outlined in Chapter 4. Most cooperatives had achieved significant livelihoods changes and benefits for the women, particularly the fair trade cooperatives. In addition, the Targanine cooperatives, which had negotiated a benefit-sharing arrangement with L'Oréal and Cognis, as well as significant supply volumes to large chains like The Body Shop, showed higher material benefit levels again (e.g. crèches, white goods, health care, travel, income, literacy programs, etc.) (examined in Chapters 3 and 4). This kind of benefit-sharing agreement is an important form of recognition for the contributions of Indigenous knowledge of bio-resources towards research and development of new products – in this case, cosmetic creams sold by L'Oréal. As the Nagoya Protocol is ratified by more countries around the world, it is likely that there will be more examples of this kind globally.

As explained in the legal geographies chapter (Chapter 3), there have also been naming and branding disputes. These are significantly linked to the cultural heritage, human bio-geographical and *terroir* that the Amazigh women producers have with the argan forest. Other companies that do not even appear to purchase oil from Morocco or produce it there, and that came across argan oil 'not through years of research', but 'by accident' (CNN, 2012; Soetan, 2012), have been successfully marketing their products as 'Moroccan Oil' or similar. This clearly seems to unfairly free-ride on the 'exoticism' of the *terroir* – the long history of the Amazigh connection to the argan tree and its unique geographical and environmental context in the arid Souss Valley and Anti-Atlas Mountains on the edge of the Sahara Desert. As a result, the Association Marocaine de l'Industrie Géographique de l'Huile d'Argane (AMIGHA) was established to register and enforce a geographical indication in Morocco and Europe. To date, this process has not succeeded in protecting a geographical indication of 'Argane', but there are ongoing initiatives and even court cases globally regarding branding surrounding names such as 'argan' and 'Moroccan argan oil' (CTB, 2010; Réviron and El Benni, 2012; WIPO, 2015).

Last, Chapter 5 celebrated the producer stories of women and their daily lives, which although hard in many ways, have brought about solidarity, well-being improvements and empowerment for Amazigh women in the cooperatives. Often, these stories are too 'ordinary' or 'mundane' to receive much uptake in economically development-oriented literature. But as Daya (2014, p. 284) explains, telling producer stories is important for 'revealing ordinary people whose economic practices are both mundane and socially rich, "materialising" and sustaining such human capacities as love, dignity, memory, friendship and kinship'. Although there remain many challenges faced by Amazigh women, the argan cooperative members that were interviewed suggested that these cooperatives were providing a place to embrace their solidarity, to support each other and share their stories. As an Indigenous majority group, the Amazigh women in the cooperatives were also receiving incremental benefits towards improved livelihoods, well-being and freedoms for women, which accords with the findings of other authors (Lybbert et al., 2011; le Polain de Waroux and Lambin, 2013). As Indigenous and women's rights reforms of the past 20 years continue to occur in Morocco (Salime, 2011; Gagliardi, 2019), the increased opportunity for women and girls to receive further formal education and literacy is likely to increase their capacity to advocate for their rights and to negotiate further freedoms. As a whole, the women's cooperatives have been receiving increasing global recognition. Through their solidarity, they stand to continue women's empowerment in the context of the other Amazigh and feminist movements in Morocco and North Africa.

References

Carr, C. and Gibson, C. (2016). Geographies of Making: Rethinking Materials and Skills for Volatile Futures. *Progress in Human Geography*, 40(3), pp. 297–315.

CNN (2012, 30 September). Made in Israel: Moroccan Oil, <https://edition.cnn.com/videos/bestoftv/2012/06/01/exp-eb-israel-moroccan-oil.cnn>.

Coole, D. and Frost, S. (2010). Introducing the New Materialisms. In D. Coole and S. Frost (eds). *New Materialisms: Ontology, Agency, and Politics* (pp. 1–43). Durham, North Carolina: Duke University Press.

CTB (Trade for Development Centre) (2010). *Huile d'argan? L'or du Maroc?* Brussels: Agence Belge de Développement.

Daya, S. (2014). Beyond Exploitation/Empowerment: Re-imagining Southern Producers in Commodity Stories. *Social & Cultural Geography*, 15(7), pp. 812–833.

Gagliardi, S. (2019). Indigenous Peoples' Rights in Morocco: Subaltern Narratives by Amazigh Women. *International Journal of Human Rights*, 23(1–2), pp. 281–296.

Head, L., Atchison, J. and Gates, A. (2012). *Ingrained. A Human Bio-Geography of Wheat*. Burlington: Ashgate.

Huang, P. (2017). Liquid Gold: Berber Women and the Argan Oil Co-operatives in Morocco. *International Journal of Intangible Heritage*, 12(1), pp. 140–155.

Ingold, T. (2000). *The Perception of the Environment: Essays on Livelihood, Dwelling and Skill*. London: Routledge.

Ingold, T. (2010) The Textility of Making. *Cambridge Journal of Economics*, 34(1), pp. 91–102.

Institut de Recherche pour le Développement (IRD).(2011). The Moroccan Arganeraie Shaped by Human Endeavour. IRD Scientific Newssheets, no. 367, <https://www.en.ird.fr/the-media-centre>, accessed 12 December 2019.

Khallouki, F., Eddouks, M., Mourad, A., Breuer, A. and Owen, R. (2017). Ethnobotanic, Ethnopharmacologic Aspects and New Phytochemical Insights into Moroccan Argan Fruits. *International Journal of Molecular Sciences*, 18(11), pp. 2277–2301.

le Polain De Waroux, Y. and Lambin, E. F. (2013). Niche Commodities and Rural Poverty Alleviation: Contextualizing the Contribution of Argan Oil to Rural Livelihoods in Morocco. *Annals of the Association of American Geographers*, 103(3), pp. 589–607.

Lybbert, T., Aboudrare, A., Chaloud, D., Magnan, N. and Nash, M. (2011). Booming Markets for Moroccan Argan Oil Appear to Benefit Some Rural Households While Threatening the Endemic Argan Forest. *Proceedings of the National Academy of Sciences*, 108(34), pp. 13963–13968.

Réviron, S. and El Benni, N. (2012). Morocco: Argan Oil. In M. Blakeney (ed.). *Extending the Protection of Geographical Indications: Case Studies of Agricultural Products in Africa* (pp. 255–265). London: Earthscan.

Ruas, M.-P., Tengberg, M., Ettahiri, A., Fili, A. and Van Staëvel, J.-P. (2011). Archaeobotanical Research at the Medieval Fortified Site of Îgîlîz (Anti-Atlas, Morocco) with Particular Reference to the Exploitation of the Argan Tree. *Vegetation History and Archaeobotany*, 20(5), pp. 419–433.

Salime, Z. (2011). *Between Feminism and Islam: Human Rights and Sharia Law in Morocco*. Minneapolis, Minnesota: University of Minnesota Press.

Soetan, F. (2012, 16 December). Mining Liquid Gold: Carmen Tal, CEO Moroccan Oil, <http://venturesafrica.com/mining-liquid-gold-carmen-tal-ceo-moroccanoil/>.

UNESCO (2014). Report on the Status of an Element Inscribed on the List of Intangible Cultural Heritage, <https://ich.unesco.org/en/RL/argan-practices-and-know-how-concerning-the-argan-tree-00955>.

World Intellectual Property Organization (WIPO) (2015). Protecting Society and the Environment with a Geographical Indication: Argan Oil Morocco. WIPO Case Studies, <https://www.wipo.int/ipadvantage/en/details.jsp?id=2656>.

Index

For Product Safety Concerns and Information please contact our EU representative GPSR@taylorandfrancis.com
Taylor & Francis Verlag GmbH, Kaufingerstraße 24, 80331 München, Germany

www.ingramcontent.com/pod-product-compliance
Lightning Source LLC
LaVergne TN
LVHW010930110826
845149LV00013B/2538

* 9 7 8 1 0 3 2 2 3 7 7 3 2 *